Table of Contents

Chapter 1: Introduction to Microsoft Office

1.1. The Evolution of Microsoft Office: A Historical Perspective

Microsoft Office has a rich history that has evolved over several decades. It all began in 1989 when Microsoft introduced the first version of Microsoft Office, which included applications like Word, Excel, and PowerPoint. This suite of productivity tools quickly became popular among businesses and individuals alike.

Early Years

In the early years, Microsoft Office primarily ran on the Windows operating system. It was a significant departure from previous software suites, as it integrated various applications seamlessly. This integration made it easier for users to work with different types of documents and data.

The Rise of Word and Excel

Word and Excel quickly emerged as the standout applications within Microsoft Office. Microsoft Word revolutionized word processing, providing users with powerful text editing and formatting capabilities. Excel, on the other hand, became the go-to spreadsheet application, enabling users to perform complex calculations and data analysis.

Office for Mac and Cross-Platform Compatibility

As Microsoft Office continued to evolve, it expanded to other platforms, including the Macintosh. This move opened up Microsoft Office to a wider user base. Cross-platform compatibility became a key focus, allowing users to collaborate across different operating systems seamlessly.

The Shift to Office 365

In recent years, Microsoft made a significant shift by introducing Office 365, a cloud-based subscription service. This marked a departure from the traditional model of purchasing standalone software licenses. Office 365 offered users the flexibility to access their favorite Office applications from anywhere with an internet connection.

Modern Collaboration Tools

With Office 365, Microsoft also introduced collaboration tools like SharePoint and Microsoft Teams. These tools enable real-time collaboration, making it easier for teams to work together on documents and projects, regardless of their physical location.

Constant Innovation

Microsoft continues to innovate, with regular updates and new features for Office 365 users. The inclusion of artificial intelligence and machine learning has made Office applications smarter and more efficient. Users can now benefit from features like real-time translation, advanced data analysis, and more.

The evolution of Microsoft Office has been remarkable, from its early days as a suite of desktop applications to its current cloud-based, collaborative incarnation. Understanding this history is essential for anyone looking to harness the full power of Microsoft Office in today's digital workplace.

1.2. Overview of Key Applications: Word, Excel, PowerPoint, and More

Microsoft Office is a suite of productivity software that includes a variety of applications, each designed for specific tasks and purposes. Understanding the key applications within Microsoft Office is essential for efficiently using the suite for various tasks. Here, we provide an overview of some of the most important applications, including Microsoft Word, Excel, PowerPoint, and others.

Microsoft Word

Microsoft Word is a word processing application used for creating and formatting documents. It is the go-to tool for tasks like writing reports, letters, essays, and other text-based documents. Word offers features for text formatting, spell checking, grammar checking, and the creation of professional-looking documents. Users can also add images, charts, tables, and other elements to enhance their documents.

To create a new document in Word:
```
1. Open Microsoft Word.
2. Click on "New Document" or press Ctrl+N.
3. Start typing your content.
4. Use the toolbar at the top to format text, insert images, and more.
5. Save your document by clicking "File" > "Save" or pressing Ctrl+S.
```

Microsoft Excel

Microsoft Excel is a spreadsheet application used for tasks involving data analysis, calculations, and visualization. Excel provides a grid-like interface known as a worksheet, where users can organize data into rows and columns. It supports formulas and functions for performing calculations, creating charts, and generating reports.

To create a simple Excel spreadsheet:
```
1. Open Microsoft Excel.
2. Click on "Blank Workbook" to start a new spreadsheet.
3. Enter data into cells by selecting a cell and typing.
4. Use formulas (e.g., =SUM(A1:A5)) for calculations.
5. Create charts by selecting data and choosing a chart type.
```

Microsoft PowerPoint

Microsoft PowerPoint is a presentation application used for creating slideshows and presentations. It allows users to create visually engaging slides with text, images, animations, and multimedia elements. PowerPoint is widely used for business presentations, educational lectures, and more.

To create a PowerPoint presentation:
1. Open Microsoft PowerPoint.
2. Choose a template or start with a blank slide.
3. Add slides by clicking "New Slide" or pressing Ctrl+M.
4. Insert text, images, and other content on each slide.
5. Use animations and transitions for visual effects.

Microsoft Outlook

Microsoft Outlook is an email and personal information management application. It is used for sending and receiving emails, managing calendars, scheduling appointments, and organizing tasks and contacts. Outlook also offers features for filtering and organizing emails.

To send an email in Outlook:
1. Open Microsoft Outlook.
2. Click on "New Email" or press Ctrl+Shift+M.
3. Enter the recipient's email address in the "To" field.
4. Type your message in the email body.
5. Click "Send" to send the email.

Other Office Applications

In addition to these key applications, Microsoft Office includes several other tools, such as:

- **Microsoft Access**: A database management application for storing and manipulating data.
- **Microsoft OneNote**: A note-taking application for capturing ideas, notes, and drawings.
- **Microsoft Publisher**: A desktop publishing application for creating brochures, newsletters, and more.
- **Microsoft Visio**: A diagramming and vector graphics application for creating flowcharts, diagrams, and schematics.

Understanding the purpose and features of each application allows users to select the most appropriate tool for their specific tasks and maximize their productivity within the Microsoft Office suite.

1.3. Navigating the Microsoft Office Interface

The Microsoft Office suite features a consistent interface across its applications, making it easier for users to navigate and work efficiently. Whether you're using Microsoft Word, Excel, PowerPoint, or other Office tools, understanding the interface elements is crucial. In this section, we'll explore the key components of the Microsoft Office interface.

The Ribbon

The **Ribbon** is a prominent feature in Office applications, containing tabs with various commands and tools. Each application has context-specific tabs that group related functions. For example, in Microsoft Word, you'll find tabs like "Home," "Insert," "Page Layout," and more. Clicking on a tab reveals a set of related commands and options.

To use the Ribbon:
1. Open any Office application.
2. Explore the tabs to find the command you need.
3. Click on a command to execute it.
4. Some commands may have dropdown menus with additional options.

Quick Access Toolbar

The **Quick Access Toolbar** is a customizable toolbar located above the Ribbon. Users can add frequently used commands to this toolbar for quick access. It's a time-saving feature, allowing you to perform common actions without navigating through the Ribbon.

To customize the Quick Access Toolbar:
1. Click the down arrow on the toolbar.
2. Select "Customize Quick Access Toolbar."
3. Choose commands to add or remove from the toolbar.
4. Click "OK" to save your changes.

Backstage View

The **Backstage View** is accessed by clicking on the "File" tab in Office applications. It provides options for managing documents, such as creating new documents, opening existing files, saving, printing, and sharing. Backstage View also offers document properties and settings.

To access the Backstage View:
1. Click on the "File" tab in any Office application.
2. Explore the options in the left-hand panel for document management tasks.
3. Make selections and changes as needed.

Document View

The main area of the Office application is the **Document View**, where you create and edit your content. This area varies depending on the application and the document type. For example, in Microsoft Word, it's where you type and format text, while in Excel, it's where you enter data and perform calculations in cells.

Status Bar

The **Status Bar** is located at the bottom of the application window and provides information about the document and current tasks. It displays word counts, page numbers, zoom settings, and more, depending on the application.

To use the Status Bar:
1. View information, such as word count, on the left side.
2. Adjust zoom settings using the slider on the right side.

Keyboard Shortcuts

Office applications offer numerous keyboard shortcuts to perform actions quickly. For example, pressing Ctrl+S in most applications will save the document. Learning these shortcuts can significantly boost your productivity.

To use keyboard shortcuts:
1. Press the appropriate key combination (e.g., Ctrl+S for saving).
2. Refer to the application's help documentation for a list of available shortcuts.

Understanding these key elements of the Microsoft Office interface will help you navigate the applications more efficiently and perform tasks with ease. Whether you're a beginner or an experienced user, mastering the interface is a fundamental step toward proficiency in Office tools.

1.4. Essential Skills for Effective Office Suite Use

To harness the full potential of Microsoft Office or any office suite, it's essential to develop certain skills that enable effective usage. These skills are not only valuable for productivity but also contribute to creating polished and professional documents, spreadsheets, presentations, and communications. In this section, we'll discuss some of the essential skills you should cultivate.

Typing Skills

One of the foundational skills for working with Microsoft Office is proficient typing. Whether you're drafting an email in Outlook, entering data in Excel, or writing a report in Word, fast and accurate typing can save you time and reduce errors. Consider practicing touch typing to improve your speed and accuracy.

Formatting and Styling

Understanding how to format and style your documents, spreadsheets, and presentations is crucial for creating visually appealing and structured content. Familiarize yourself with features like font selection, paragraph spacing, bullet points, and numbering to enhance the readability of your documents.

Basic Math and Formulas

In Excel, basic math skills are essential for performing calculations. You should be comfortable with addition, subtraction, multiplication, and division. Additionally, learn how to create and use formulas to automate calculations. Functions like SUM, AVERAGE, and IF are fundamental for data analysis.

```
Example of a simple Excel formula:
=SUM(A1:A5)  // Calculates the sum of values in cells A1 to A5.
```

Data Organization

Efficient data organization is crucial, especially when dealing with large datasets in Excel or databases in Access. Learn how to structure your data logically, use headers and labels, and create tables when necessary. Properly organized data simplifies analysis and reporting.

Mastering Styles and Templates

In applications like Word and PowerPoint, mastering styles and templates can save you a significant amount of time. Create custom styles for consistent document formatting and design templates for presentations to maintain a professional look and feel across your work.

Collaboration and Version Control

Collaboration skills are vital in a professional setting. Learn how to collaborate on documents and spreadsheets in real-time using tools like Office 365's co-authoring features. Understand version control to track changes and manage revisions effectively.

Problem-Solving and Troubleshooting

No matter how skilled you are, issues can arise. Develop problem-solving and troubleshooting skills to address unexpected errors or challenges that may occur while working with Office applications. Explore online resources and forums for assistance when needed.

Time Management

Effective time management is crucial when working with Office applications. Plan your tasks, set deadlines, and prioritize work to optimize your productivity. Consider using tools like Outlook's calendar and task management features to stay organized.

Continuous Learning

Microsoft Office is constantly evolving, with new features and updates. Dedicate time to continuous learning by exploring new features, attending training sessions, and staying up-to-date with Office-related news. This ensures that you make the most of the suite's capabilities.

Documentation and Training

As you acquire these essential skills, consider documenting your knowledge and creating training materials. This not only helps reinforce your understanding but also allows you to share your expertise with colleagues or team members, fostering a collaborative environment.

By cultivating these essential skills, you'll be better equipped to work efficiently and effectively within the Microsoft Office suite, contributing to your personal and professional growth.

1.5. Setting Up and Customizing Your Workspace

Customizing your workspace in Microsoft Office can greatly enhance your productivity and make your workflow more efficient. Whether you're using Word, Excel, PowerPoint, or any other Office application, setting up your workspace to suit your preferences can save time and reduce distractions. In this section, we'll explore various ways to personalize and optimize your Office environment.

User Account and Sign-In

To access personalized settings and cloud-based features in Office, it's essential to sign in with a Microsoft account or an Office 365 account. This allows you to save documents to the cloud, access your settings across devices, and collaborate with others in real-time.

```
To sign in to Office:
1. Open any Office application.
2. Click on "Sign In" or "Account" in the application's menu.
3. Enter your Microsoft or Office 365 account credentials.
4. Follow the on-screen instructions to complete the sign-in process.
```

Customizing the Ribbon

The Ribbon in Office applications can be customized to display the commands and tools you use most frequently. You can add or remove tabs, create custom tabs, and rearrange commands to create a Ribbon that suits your workflow.

```
To customize the Ribbon:
1. Right-click on the Ribbon and choose "Customize the Ribbon."
2. In the "Customize the Ribbon" dialog, customize tab names and add or remov
e commands.
3. Click "OK" to apply your changes.
```

Themes and Backgrounds

Personalize your Office experience by changing the theme and background. You can choose from different color schemes and background images to match your preferences. Themes affect the overall appearance of Office applications.

To change the Office theme:
1. Go to "File" > "Options" (or "Preferences" on a Mac).
2. In the "General" or "Personalization" section, select your desired theme.
3. Click "OK" to apply the theme changes.

AutoSave and AutoRecover

Enable AutoSave and AutoRecover features to automatically save your work and recover it in case of unexpected shutdowns or crashes. This ensures that you don't lose your progress when working on important documents.

To enable AutoSave and AutoRecover:
1. Go to "File" > "Options" (or "Preferences" on a Mac).
2. In the options dialog, select "Save" or "Save & Backup."
3. Configure AutoSave and AutoRecover settings as desired.

Custom Templates

Create and use custom templates in Office applications to streamline document creation. You can design templates for reports, presentations, and other recurring tasks. Custom templates ensure consistency in your work.

To create a custom template:
1. Create a document with the desired layout and formatting.
2. Save the document as a template (e.g., .dotx for Word, .potx for PowerPoint).
3. Access the template from the "New" or "New Document" options in the application.

Keyboard Shortcuts

Customize keyboard shortcuts to perform actions more quickly. If there are specific commands you use frequently, assign custom key combinations to them for instant access.

To customize keyboard shortcuts:
1. Go to "File" > "Options" (or "Preferences" on a Mac).
2. In the options dialog, select "Customize Ribbon" or "Keyboard Shortcuts."
3. Create or modify keyboard shortcuts as needed.

Add-Ins and Extensions

Explore the Office Store to find add-ins and extensions that enhance your Office experience. These third-party tools can provide additional functionality and integration with other apps and services.

To install Office add-ins:
1. Go to "Insert" > "Get Add-ins" (in some Office applications).
2. Browse or search for the desired add-in.
3. Click "Add" or "Install" to add the extension to your Office environment.

Customizing your Office workspace according to your needs and preferences can make a significant difference in your productivity and overall user experience. By following these customization tips, you can create a workspace that enhances your efficiency and fits your unique workflow.

Chapter 2: Mastering Microsoft Word

2.1. Creating and Formatting Documents

Microsoft Word is a powerful word processing application that allows you to create and format documents of various types. Whether you're writing a report, a letter, an essay, or any other type of document, mastering the basics of creating and formatting in Word is essential. In this section, we'll explore the fundamental steps for creating and formatting documents in Microsoft Word.

Creating a New Document

To create a new document in Microsoft Word, follow these simple steps:

1. **Open Microsoft Word**: Launch Microsoft Word by clicking on its icon in your Start menu (Windows) or Applications folder (Mac). You can also open Word by searching for it in the Windows search bar or using Spotlight on Mac.

2. **Choose a Template (Optional)**: Word offers various templates for different types of documents, such as resumes, letters, and reports. You can start with a blank document or select a template that matches your document's purpose.

3. **Begin Typing**: Once you have a new document open, you can start typing your content. The blinking cursor indicates where your text will appear.

Basic Text Formatting

Microsoft Word provides a range of formatting options to make your text visually appealing and easy to read. Here are some common text formatting tasks:

- **Font Style and Size**: You can change the font style and size using the formatting toolbar at the top. Highlight the text you want to format and select the desired font and font size.

- **Bold, Italic, and Underline**: You can make text bold, italic, or underline by selecting the respective formatting options from the toolbar or using keyboard shortcuts (e.g., Ctrl+B for bold).

- **Alignment**: Adjust the alignment of your text (left, center, right, or justified) using the alignment options on the toolbar.

- **Bullet Points and Numbered Lists**: Create bulleted or numbered lists by clicking the respective icons on the toolbar.

- **Text Color and Highlighting**: Change the text color and apply highlighting by using the color options on the toolbar.

Paragraph Formatting

In addition to text formatting, you can also format paragraphs in Microsoft Word:

- **Line Spacing**: Adjust line spacing between paragraphs using options like single spacing, double spacing, or custom spacing.

- **Paragraph Indentation**: Set paragraph indentation for the first line or entire paragraphs using the indentation options.

- **Alignment**: Change paragraph alignment, such as left-align, center, right-align, or justified alignment.

- **Spacing Before and After**: Control the spacing before and after paragraphs to improve document readability.

Page Layout

Microsoft Word allows you to customize the page layout for your document:

- **Margins**: Adjust the margins (the space around the edges of the page) to control how content fits on the page.

- **Page Orientation**: Choose between portrait (vertical) and landscape (horizontal) page orientation.

- **Page Size**: Change the page size to fit different paper formats (e.g., letter, legal, A4).

- **Page Breaks**: Insert page breaks to control where a new page starts within your document.

Saving and Printing

To save your document, click on the "File" tab, select "Save" or "Save As," and choose the location where you want to save the file. Give your document a meaningful name and select the file format (e.g., .docx).

To print your document, click on the "File" tab, select "Print," and configure the printing options, such as selecting the printer, choosing the number of copies, and setting page ranges.

By mastering these basics of creating and formatting documents in Microsoft Word, you'll be well-equipped to create polished and professional-looking documents for various purposes. Word offers a wide range of advanced formatting features and tools, but these fundamentals serve as a strong foundation for your word processing tasks.

2.2. Advanced Text Editing Techniques

In Microsoft Word, advanced text editing techniques can help you work efficiently and make your documents more polished. These techniques go beyond basic formatting and involve features like document navigation, search and replace, and managing document elements. In this section, we'll explore some of these advanced text editing techniques.

Document Navigation

When working on long documents, efficient navigation is crucial. Here are some ways to navigate your document effectively:

- **Navigation Pane**: Use the Navigation Pane to quickly jump to different sections, headings, or search for specific text. You can open the Navigation Pane by clicking on "View" and selecting "Navigation Pane."

- **Go To**: The "Go To" feature allows you to navigate to a specific page, section, or line in your document. Press Ctrl+G or go to "Edit" > "Go To" to access this feature.

Find and Replace

Finding and replacing text is a powerful feature in Word that can save you a lot of time when editing your document. Here's how to use it:

- **Find**: To find specific text in your document, press Ctrl+F or go to "Edit" > "Find." Enter the text you want to find, and Word will locate the first occurrence.

- **Replace**: To replace text, use the "Replace" feature. Press Ctrl+H or go to "Edit" > "Replace." Enter the text to find and the replacement text. You can replace one occurrence at a time or replace all occurrences in the document.

Advanced Copy and Paste

When copying and pasting text, you can use advanced options to control how the text is pasted:

- **Paste Special**: Instead of a regular paste (Ctrl+V), you can choose "Paste Special" from the context menu to paste text as unformatted text, HTML, or other formats.

- **Clipboard Pane**: The Clipboard Pane allows you to copy multiple items and then choose which one to paste. Click the "Clipboard" icon in the Home tab to open the Clipboard Pane.

Styles and Themes

Using styles and themes can help maintain consistency in your document's formatting:

- **Styles:** Apply predefined styles to headings, paragraphs, and other elements in your document. This ensures uniform formatting and makes it easier to update the document's look later. Access styles in the "Styles" group on the Home tab.

- **Themes**: Themes provide a consistent color scheme, font set, and overall design for your document. You can choose a theme from the "Design" tab.

Track Changes

When collaborating on a document or receiving feedback, you can enable "Track Changes" to keep a record of edits and comments:

- **Track Changes**: Go to the "Review" tab and enable "Track Changes" to mark any additions, deletions, or formatting changes made to the document. Comments can be added to provide feedback.

- **Accept/Reject Changes**: Review changes and choose to accept or reject them individually or all at once.

Document Protection

To protect your document from unauthorized changes or to limit editing, you can use document protection features:

- **Document Password**: You can set a password to restrict access to the document. Go to "File" > "Info" > "Protect Document" > "Encrypt with Password" to set a password.

- **Restrict Editing**: You can restrict editing by allowing only certain types of changes. Go to "Review" > "Protect" > "Restrict Editing" to configure editing restrictions.

Advanced Find and Replace with Wildcards

If you need to find and replace text with specific patterns, you can use wildcards in your search queries. This allows for more complex search and replace operations. To enable wildcards in the Find and Replace dialog, click "More" > "Use wildcards."

Mastering these advanced text editing techniques in Microsoft Word can significantly improve your efficiency and document management skills. Whether you're working on a complex project or simply want to enhance your proficiency, these features will help you tackle various editing tasks with ease.

2.3. Working with Templates and Styles

Templates and styles are powerful tools in Microsoft Word that allow you to maintain consistency, save time, and create professional-looking documents. Templates provide pre-designed layouts for various document types, while styles enable consistent formatting throughout your document. In this section, we'll delve into working with templates and styles in Microsoft Word.

Using Templates

Templates serve as the foundation for your document's layout and design. Microsoft Word offers a wide range of built-in templates for different document types, such as resumes, newsletters, brochures, and more. Here's how to use templates:

1. **Select a Template**: Open Word and click on "File" > "New." Browse through the available templates and select the one that suits your document's purpose.

2. **Customize Content**: After selecting a template, you can customize the text and content to match your specific needs. Simply click on the placeholder text and replace it with your own.

3. **Modify Styles (Optional)**: Templates often come with predefined styles. You can modify these styles to change fonts, colors, and formatting to match your preferences. Use the "Styles" pane to manage styles.

4. **Save Your Document**: Once you've customized the template, save it with a new name to create your unique document. Go to "File" > "Save As" and choose a location to save your document.

Creating Your Own Templates

If you frequently use a specific layout or design for your documents, you can create your own custom templates. Here's how:

1. **Design Your Document**: Create a new document and format it according to your preferences. Add headers, footers, fonts, and any other elements you want to include in your template.

2. **Save as Template**: Go to "File" > "Save As." Choose "Word Template" from the file format options and give your template a name. Save it in the Templates folder for easy access.

3. **Use Your Custom Template**: To use your custom template, click on "File" > "New" and select "Personal" or "Custom" templates. You'll find your template there.

Working with Styles

Styles in Word enable consistent formatting throughout your document. They define the font, size, color, and other formatting attributes for different elements like headings, paragraphs, and lists. Here's how to work with styles:

1. **Apply Styles**: Highlight the text you want to format with a specific style, and then select the style from the "Styles" pane on the Home tab. Styles can also be applied using keyboard shortcuts.

2. **Modify Styles**: To change the appearance of a style, right-click the style in the "Styles" pane and select "Modify." Make the desired changes to the font, size, color, or other formatting options.

3. **Create Custom Styles**: You can create your own custom styles for specialized formatting needs. Click the "New Style" button in the "Styles" pane and define the formatting options.

4. **Manage Styles**: The "Styles" pane allows you to manage styles, including deleting, renaming, or organizing them into style sets.

Quick Style Sets

Word provides Quick Style Sets that are predefined combinations of fonts and colors. These sets offer a quick way to change the overall look of your document. To apply a Quick Style Set, go to the "Design" tab and select one from the available options.

Style Inspector

The Style Inspector is a useful tool for checking and troubleshooting styles in your document. It allows you to see which styles are applied to specific text and adjust them if needed. You can access the Style Inspector from the "Home" tab under the "Styles" group.

By mastering templates and styles in Microsoft Word, you can create professional documents with consistent formatting and save time on repetitive tasks. Whether you're using built-in templates, customizing them, or designing your own templates and styles, these tools are essential for efficient document creation and formatting.

2.4. Incorporating Graphics and Tables

Incorporating graphics and tables into your Microsoft Word documents can greatly enhance their visual appeal and effectiveness in conveying information. Whether you're adding images, charts, or tables, it's essential to know how to insert, format, and manage these elements within your document. In this section, we'll explore the process of incorporating graphics and tables into your Word documents.

Inserting Images

Adding images to your document can make it more engaging and informative. To insert images:

1. **Place the Cursor**: Position your cursor at the location in the document where you want to insert the image.

2. **Insert Image**: Go to the "Insert" tab and click on "Pictures." Select the image file you want to insert from your computer. Alternatively, you can copy an image from another source (e.g., a web page or another document) and paste it directly into your document.

3. **Resize and Move**: After inserting the image, you can resize it by clicking and dragging the corners. To move the image, click and drag it to the desired location within the document.

4. **Image Formatting**: The "Format" tab will appear when the image is selected, allowing you to adjust settings such as image styles, borders, and effects.

Adding Charts and Graphs

Charts and graphs are useful for presenting data visually. To add a chart:

1. **Place the Cursor**: Position your cursor where you want to insert the chart.

2. **Insert Chart**: Go to the "Insert" tab and click on "Chart." Select the chart type that suits your data, and Excel will open with a sample data table.

3. **Enter Data**: Replace the sample data in Excel with your own dataset. The chart in Word will automatically update to reflect the changes.

4. **Format Chart**: Use the "Chart Design" and "Format" tabs to format the chart's appearance, labels, and other elements.

Creating Tables

Tables are effective for organizing and presenting information in a structured manner. To create a table:

1. **Place the Cursor**: Position your cursor where you want to insert the table.

2. **Insert Table**: Go to the "Insert" tab and click on "Table." You can either draw the table's dimensions or select the number of rows and columns from the grid.

3. **Enter Data**: Click within each cell to enter text or data. You can also use keyboard shortcuts like Tab and Enter to navigate through cells.

4. **Table Design**: The "Table Design" tab allows you to format the table's appearance, including styles, borders, shading, and alignment.

5. **Table Tools**: When you select the table, the "Table Tools" tab appears, providing options for working with rows, columns, and cells, as well as sorting and calculating data.

SmartArt Graphics

SmartArt graphics in Word enable you to create diagrams, flowcharts, and organizational charts. To insert SmartArt:

1. **Place the Cursor**: Position your cursor where you want to insert the SmartArt graphic.

2. **Insert SmartArt**: Go to the "Insert" tab and click on "SmartArt." Choose a SmartArt graphic category and select the specific graphic that suits your needs.

3. **Enter Text**: In the SmartArt pane that appears, enter text into each shape or box to customize the graphic. You can also add or remove shapes as needed.

4. **SmartArt Design**: The "SmartArt Design" and "Format" tabs provide options to change the layout, style, color scheme, and other aspects of the SmartArt graphic.

WordArt

WordArt allows you to create stylized text with effects like shadows, gradients, and 3D formatting. To insert WordArt:

1. **Place the Cursor**: Position your cursor where you want to insert the WordArt text.

2. **Insert WordArt**: Go to the "Insert" tab and click on "WordArt." Choose a WordArt style and enter your text in the pop-up box.

3. **Formatting WordArt**: After inserting WordArt, you can format it using the "Format" tab, where you can adjust text fill, outline, and effects.

Incorporating graphics and tables into your Word documents enhances their visual appeal and helps convey information more effectively. Whether you're using images, charts, tables, SmartArt graphics, or WordArt, Word provides a range of tools and formatting options to make your documents engaging and informative.

2.5. Document Collaboration and Review

Collaboration and reviewing are essential aspects of creating high-quality documents in Microsoft Word, especially when working on projects with multiple contributors or when seeking feedback and approval. In this section, we'll explore the tools and techniques available in Word for document collaboration and review.

Sharing and Collaborating

Microsoft Word offers several ways to collaborate on a document with others:

1. **Sharing via Cloud Services**: One of the most common methods is to save your document in a cloud storage service like OneDrive or SharePoint. This allows you to share a link to the document with collaborators, and multiple people can edit it simultaneously in real-time using Office Online.

2. **Email Collaboration**: You can also send a copy of the document via email and enable email collaboration. When you share the document, recipients can edit it without the need for a Microsoft account.

3. **Co-Authoring**: When working on a document stored in a shared location (e.g., OneDrive), multiple users can collaborate simultaneously. Each collaborator's changes are tracked and merged in real-time.

Tracking Changes

Tracking changes is a fundamental feature for reviewing and editing documents. To enable track changes:

1. **Review Tab**: Go to the "Review" tab and click on "Track Changes" to enable this feature. Once it's activated, any changes made to the document will be marked and attributed to the specific user.

2. **Editing and Reviewing**: Collaborators can make edits, insert comments, and suggest changes while track changes is active. All these modifications are visible to others.

3. **Accept and Reject Changes**: The author or document owner can review and decide whether to accept or reject each change individually or collectively. This is done through the "Review" tab.

4. **Comments**: Collaborators can add comments to the document to provide explanations, clarifications, or suggestions. Comments can be marked as resolved once the issue is addressed.

Comparing Documents

Comparing two versions of a document is useful for identifying changes and differences. Word allows you to compare documents as follows:

1. **Review Tab**: Go to the "Review" tab and click on "Compare" in the "Compare" group. Select "Compare" again in the dropdown menu.

2. **Original and Revised Documents**: Choose the original document and the revised document. Word will generate a comparison document showing the changes, deletions, and insertions.

3. **Review Changes**: Review the comparison document to see the differences clearly highlighted. You can accept or reject changes as needed.

Protecting and Restricting Editing

To maintain document integrity, you can protect it from unwanted changes or restrict editing to specific parts of the document:

1. **Protect Document**: Go to the "Review" tab and click on "Protect Document." You can choose to restrict formatting, editing, or comments. Set a password if necessary.

2. **Restrict Editing**: You can also restrict editing to specific parts of the document using "Restrict Editing" options. This allows you to designate certain sections as "Read-Only" or specify which users can edit specific parts.

Document Comments and Annotations

Document comments and annotations are helpful for providing feedback and clarifications within the document:

1. **Insert Comments**: Highlight the text you want to comment on, right-click, and select "New Comment." Add your comment, and it will appear as a bubble in the document's margin.

2. **Annotations**: Use the "Ink" tool to make annotations or freehand drawings directly on the document. This is particularly useful for touch-enabled devices or tablets.

Collaborating and reviewing documents efficiently is crucial for maintaining accuracy and quality. Microsoft Word's collaboration and reviewing features, including sharing, track changes, comments, document comparison, and protection, streamline the process of working on documents with others, ensuring that everyone can contribute effectively while maintaining document integrity.

Chapter 3: Excel Essentials

3.1. Spreadsheet Basics: Creating and Formatting

Microsoft Excel is a powerful spreadsheet application that is widely used for tasks ranging from simple data entry to complex calculations and data analysis. In this section, we'll explore the basics of creating and formatting spreadsheets in Excel.

Creating a New Workbook

When you open Excel, you're working with a workbook. A workbook is like a container for your spreadsheets. To create a new workbook:

1. **Open Excel**: Launch Microsoft Excel from your computer.

2. **Create a New Workbook**: You can create a new workbook by clicking on "File" > "New" and then selecting "Blank Workbook." Alternatively, you can use the keyboard shortcut Ctrl+N.

Working with Worksheets

A workbook consists of one or more worksheets (also called sheets). Worksheets are where you enter and organize your data. By default, a new workbook contains one worksheet, but you can add more if needed:

1. **Add a New Worksheet**: To add a new worksheet, click the "+" button next to the existing worksheet tabs at the bottom of the Excel window.

2. **Rename Worksheets**: Double-click on a worksheet tab to rename it to something more meaningful.

3. **Switch Between Worksheets**: Click on the worksheet tabs to switch between different worksheets within the same workbook.

Entering Data

Entering data in Excel is straightforward. Click on a cell (the intersection of a row and a column) and start typing. Excel automatically moves to the next cell when you press Enter. Here are some key tips for entering data:

- **Editing Cells**: Double-click on a cell to edit its contents.

- **Copying and Pasting**: Use Ctrl+C to copy selected cells and Ctrl+V to paste them elsewhere.

- **Fill Handle**: Drag the fill handle (a small square at the bottom-right corner of a selected cell) to fill adjacent cells with a series or pattern.

Formatting Cells

Formatting cells in Excel allows you to change their appearance and behavior. To format cells:

1. **Select Cells**: Click and drag to select the cells you want to format.

2. **Right-Click Menu**: Right-click on the selected cells and choose "Format Cells" from the context menu.

3. **Home Tab**: You can also use the "Home" tab on the Excel ribbon to access common formatting options like font, fill color, and number format.

Cell Formatting Options

Excel offers various cell formatting options, including:

- **Font**: You can change the font style, size, color, and effects (bold, italic, underline) for selected cells.

- **Alignment**: Adjust text alignment (left, center, right) and orientation within cells.

- **Number Format**: Set the format for numbers, dates, and times, including currency symbols and decimal places.

- **Fill Color and Borders**: Apply background fill color and add borders to cells to improve readability and aesthetics.

- **Cell Styles**: Use predefined cell styles for a consistent and professional look.

Data Validation

Data validation helps ensure that the data entered into cells meets specific criteria. To apply data validation:

1. **Select Cells**: Choose the cells where you want to apply data validation.

2. **Data Validation**: Go to the "Data" tab and click on "Data Validation."

3. **Criteria**: Specify the criteria for valid data, such as whole numbers, dates within a range, or items from a list.

Managing Rows and Columns

To manage rows and columns in Excel:

- **Insert Rows/Columns**: Right-click on the row or column header and select "Insert" to add a new row or column.

- **Delete Rows/Columns**: Right-click on the row or column header and select "Delete" to remove a row or column.

- **Hide Rows/Columns**: Select the rows or columns you want to hide, right-click, and choose "Hide."

- **Freeze Panes**: To keep specific rows or columns visible while scrolling, use the "Freeze Panes" feature under the "View" tab.

Excel's spreadsheet basics involve creating and formatting worksheets, entering data, and applying various formatting options. These skills form the foundation for more advanced tasks like data analysis, chart creation, and formula usage, which we'll explore in subsequent sections of this chapter.

3.2. Formulas and Functions: The Heart of Excel

Formulas and functions are the core of Excel's power, allowing you to perform calculations, manipulate data, and automate tasks. In this section, we'll delve into the world of Excel formulas and functions, exploring their use and versatility.

Excel Formulas

Formulas in Excel are expressions that perform calculations using values, references, and operators. Formulas always start with an equal sign (=). For example, the formula "=A1+B1" adds the values in cells A1 and B1.

Here are some key aspects of Excel formulas:

- **Operators**: Excel supports various operators for arithmetic (+, -, *, /), comparison (=, <, >, <=, >=, <>), and more.

- **Cell References**: You can reference other cells in formulas using their cell addresses, such as A1, B2, or C3.

- **Functions**: Functions are predefined formulas that simplify complex calculations. For example, the SUM function calculates the sum of a range of cells.

- **Order of Operations**: Excel follows the standard order of operations (BODMAS/BIDMAS), so you can use parentheses to control the order of calculation.

Excel Functions

Excel provides a wide range of built-in functions to perform specific tasks and calculations. Functions save time and ensure accuracy in your spreadsheets. Some commonly used functions include:

- **SUM**: Adds up all the numbers in a range of cells. For example, "=SUM(A1:A5)" adds the numbers in cells A1 through A5.

- **AVERAGE**: Calculates the average of a range of numbers.

- **MIN/MAX**: Finds the minimum or maximum value in a range.

- **COUNT/COUNTA**: Counts the number of cells that contain data (COUNT) or any value, including text (COUNTA).

- **IF**: Performs conditional logic. It returns one value if a condition is true and another if it's false. For example, "=IF(A1>10,"Yes", "No")" checks if A1 is greater than 10.

- **VLOOKUP/HLOOKUP**: Searches for a value in a table and returns a corresponding value from the same row (VLOOKUP) or column (HLOOKUP).

- **INDEX/MATCH**: Retrieves a value from a specific row and column intersection in a table based on criteria (INDEX and MATCH are often used together).

- **CONCATENATE/TEXTJOIN**: Combines text from multiple cells into one cell.

Using Functions in Formulas

To use functions in formulas, follow these steps:

1. **Start with "="**: Begin the formula with an equal sign (=).

2. **Enter the Function Name**: Type the name of the function you want to use, followed by an opening parenthesis "(".

3. **Add Arguments**: Enter the function's arguments (values, cell references, or expressions) separated by commas.

4. **Close Parenthesis**: Complete the function with a closing parenthesis ")".

Here's an example using the SUM function: "=SUM(A1:A5)" calculates the sum of values in cells A1 through A5.

AutoSum

The AutoSum feature simplifies the process of applying basic functions. To use AutoSum:

1. **Select a Cell**: Click on the cell where you want the result to appear.

2. **Click AutoSum**: Go to the "Formulas" tab and click on the "AutoSum" dropdown. Choose the function you want to use (e.g., SUM, AVERAGE, COUNT).

3. **Select the Range**: Excel will suggest a range based on nearby data. Review and adjust the range if needed by clicking and dragging.

4. **Press Enter**: Hit Enter to complete the formula and calculate the result.

Excel's formulas and functions make it a versatile tool for various calculations and data manipulation tasks. Whether you're performing basic arithmetic, complex statistical analysis, or data lookup, Excel provides a function or formula to meet your needs.

Understanding how to use these tools effectively is fundamental to becoming proficient in Excel.

3.3. Data Analysis and Visualization

Data analysis and visualization are crucial aspects of Excel that enable you to gain insights from your data and present it in a meaningful way. In this section, we'll explore the tools and techniques for data analysis and visualization in Excel.

Sorting and Filtering Data

Excel provides features for sorting and filtering data to help you organize and analyze information effectively.

- **Sorting**: To sort data, select the range you want to sort and go to the "Data" tab. Click on "Sort" and choose the sorting options (ascending or descending) based on a specific column.

- **Filtering**: To filter data, select the range and click on "Filter" in the "Data" tab. You can then use filter arrows to select specific values to display in the data set.

PivotTables

PivotTables are powerful tools for summarizing and analyzing data in a dynamic way. They allow you to create custom views of your data by dragging and dropping fields.

To create a PivotTable:

1. Select your data range.

2. Go to the "Insert" tab and click on "PivotTable."

3. Choose the location for the PivotTable and click "OK."

4. Use the PivotTable Field List to select fields for rows, columns, values, and filters.

PivotTables are highly customizable and allow you to perform various calculations like sum, average, count, and more on your data.

Charts and Graphs

Excel offers a wide range of chart types to visualize data effectively. Here's how to create a chart:

1. Select your data range.

2. Go to the "Insert" tab and click on the desired chart type (e.g., bar chart, line chart, pie chart).

3. Customize the chart by adding titles, labels, and other elements.

Charts can be further customized by changing colors, styles, and data series. They provide a visual representation of your data, making it easier to identify trends and patterns.

Data Tables in Excel allow you to perform "What-If" analysis by changing one or more input values and observing the impact on calculated results. They are often used for financial modeling and scenario analysis.

To create a Data Table:

1. Set up your calculations in a worksheet, including the formula you want to analyze.

2. Choose a cell where you want to display the result.

3. Go to the "Data" tab and click on "What-If Analysis" > "Data Table."

4. Specify the row input cell (the cell containing the input values you want to change) and the column input cell (the cell containing different values to substitute).

Excel will automatically create a table with calculated results for various input values.

Goal Seek and Solver are tools for solving complex problems and optimizing values in Excel.

- **Goal Seek**: Allows you to find the input value needed to achieve a desired result. Go to "Data" > "What-If Analysis" > "Goal Seek" and specify the desired result, changing cell, and input cell.

- **Solver**: Provides more advanced optimization capabilities. It's used for problems with multiple variables and constraints. Go to "Data" > "What-If Analysis" > "Solver" to set up and solve optimization problems.

The Data Analysis ToolPak is an Excel add-in that provides additional data analysis tools, such as regression analysis, histogram creation, and moving averages.

To enable the Data Analysis ToolPak:

1. Go to "File" > "Options."

2. In the Excel Options dialog box, select "Add-Ins."

3. In the Add-Ins window, select "Analysis ToolPak" and click "OK."

Once enabled, you can access the ToolPak's functions from the "Data" tab.

Excel's data analysis and visualization features are essential for gaining insights from your data, making informed decisions, and presenting your findings effectively. Whether you're sorting, filtering, using PivotTables, creating charts, performing What-If analysis, or utilizing advanced tools like Solver and the Data Analysis ToolPak, Excel provides a wide array of options to meet your data analysis needs.

3.4. Managing Large Data Sets

Excel is a powerful tool for handling large data sets, but working with extensive amounts of data can be challenging without the right techniques. In this section, we'll explore strategies and features in Excel for efficiently managing large data sets.

Data Tables and Naming Ranges

When dealing with large data sets, it's essential to structure your data efficiently. Data tables and named ranges help organize and manage data effectively.

- **Data Tables**: Convert your data range into a table by selecting it and pressing Ctrl+T or going to the "Insert" tab and clicking "Table." Tables automatically expand when you add new data, making it easier to work with large sets.

- **Named Ranges**: Assign names to specific data ranges to simplify formulas. Select the data range, go to the "Formulas" tab, and click "Define Name" to give it a name.

Filtering and Slicing Data

Filtering and slicing data are crucial for focusing on specific portions of a large data set:

- **Filtering**: Use the "Filter" feature (under the "Data" tab) to display only the rows that meet specific criteria. This makes it easier to work with a subset of data.

- **Slicers**: Slicers are visual filtering tools that allow you to filter data in PivotTables and PivotCharts easily. To insert a slicer, click inside a PivotTable or PivotChart and go to the "Insert" tab, then click "Slicer."

PivotTables and PivotCharts

PivotTables and PivotCharts are indispensable for summarizing and analyzing large data sets:

- **PivotTables**: Create PivotTables to aggregate and summarize data quickly. Drag and drop fields to create custom views of your data. PivotTables are dynamic and update when you change the source data.

- **PivotCharts**: PivotCharts provide visual representations of PivotTable data. They allow you to create various chart types to illustrate trends and patterns in your data.

Data Consolidation

Consolidating data from multiple sources or sheets is common when dealing with large data sets. Excel offers several methods for data consolidation:

- **Consolidate Function**: Use the "Consolidate" function to combine data from multiple ranges into a single summary. Go to "Data" > "Consolidate" and follow the wizard.

- **Power Query**: Power Query is a powerful tool for importing, transforming, and combining data from different sources. It's particularly useful when working with large and complex data sets.

Data Validation and Error Checking

Data validation helps ensure data accuracy and consistency:

- **Data Validation Rules**: Set rules and restrictions for data entry to prevent errors. Go to "Data" > "Data Validation" to create rules based on criteria like dates, numbers, or custom formulas.

- **Error Checking**: Excel's error checking features can help identify and correct common errors, such as formula errors or inconsistencies in data.

Using 64-Bit Excel

If you're working with extremely large data sets, consider using the 64-bit version of Excel if it's available. The 64-bit version can handle larger data sets and use more memory compared to the 32-bit version.

To check your Excel version and switch to 64-bit if necessary:

1. Go to "File" > "Account."

2. Under "About Excel," check the version (32-bit or 64-bit).

3. If you have a 64-bit version, it will be indicated. If not, you may need to reinstall Excel using the 64-bit installer.

Data Analysis Add-Ins

Excel offers various add-ins and tools for data analysis. These add-ins provide advanced functionality for managing and analyzing large data sets. Some popular add-ins include:

- **Analysis ToolPak**: Provides statistical, financial, and engineering functions for data analysis.

- **Power Pivot**: A data modeling tool that enhances data analysis and manipulation capabilities in Excel.

- **Power Query**: Allows you to connect, transform, and load data from various sources.

When dealing with large data sets, using these add-ins can significantly improve your efficiency and analytical capabilities.

Efficiently managing large data sets in Excel requires a combination of organizing data effectively, using filtering and slicing techniques, leveraging PivotTables and PivotCharts, consolidating data from multiple sources, and taking advantage of data validation and error checking features. Additionally, considering the use of 64-bit Excel and data analysis add-ins can further enhance your ability to work with extensive data.

3.5. Excel Macros and Advanced Tools

Excel offers advanced tools and features, including macros, that can streamline tasks, automate processes, and enhance your productivity. In this section, we'll explore Excel macros and some advanced tools that can take your spreadsheet skills to the next level.

Macros in Excel

A macro is a recorded set of actions that can be played back to automate repetitive tasks. Macros are written in VBA (Visual Basic for Applications) and allow you to create custom functions, automate data processing, and perform complex tasks in Excel.

To create a simple macro:

1. Go to the "View" tab and click on "Macros."

2. Select "Record Macro."

3. Give your macro a name and assign it to a button or keyboard shortcut.

4. Perform the actions you want to record.

5. Stop recording the macro.

You can now play back the macro anytime you need to repeat those actions.

Visual Basic for Applications (VBA)

VBA is a programming language built into Excel that allows you to write custom code to automate tasks, create user-defined functions, and extend Excel's functionality. With VBA, you have full control over Excel and can create complex applications.

Here's a simple example of a VBA macro that displays a message box when a button is clicked:

```
Sub ShowMessage()
    MsgBox "Hello, Excel VBA!"
End Sub
```

You can access the VBA editor by pressing Alt+F11. From there, you can write, edit, and debug your VBA code.

Excel allows you to create custom functions using VBA. These user-defined functions (UDFs) can be used in your formulas, just like built-in Excel functions.

Here's an example of a simple UDF that calculates the factorial of a number:

```
Function Factorial(n As Integer) As Long
    If n <= 1 Then
        Factorial = 1
    Else
        Factorial = n * Factorial(n - 1)
    End If
End Function
```

You can then use this custom function in a cell like any other Excel function: =Factorial(5).

Excel add-ins are extensions that provide additional functionality and tools. Some add-ins are built into Excel, while others can be installed separately. Add-ins can enhance your productivity and offer specialized features.

To manage Excel add-ins:

1. Go to "File" > "Options."

2. Select "Add-Ins."

3. In the Add-Ins window, you can enable or disable various add-ins and manage their settings.

Solver is an Excel add-in that helps you find optimal solutions to complex problems by adjusting variables based on specified constraints. It's particularly useful for scenarios involving resource allocation, financial modeling, and optimization.

To enable the Solver add-in:

1. Go to "File" > "Options."

2. Select "Add-Ins."

3. In the Add-Ins window, check "Solver Add-In" and click "OK."

You can then access Solver from the "Data" tab.

Analysis ToolPak Add-In

The Analysis ToolPak is another Excel add-in that provides advanced data analysis and statistical functions. It's useful for performing complex statistical analysis, regression, and more.

To enable the Analysis ToolPak add-in:

1. Go to "File" > "Options."

2. Select "Add-Ins."

3. In the Add-Ins window, check "Analysis ToolPak" and click "OK."

You can access ToolPak functions from the "Data" tab.

Power Query and Power Pivot

Power Query and Power Pivot are advanced tools for data transformation and modeling in Excel. They allow you to import data from various sources, shape and clean data, and build data models for complex analysis.

Power Query and Power Pivot are often used for working with large data sets, combining data from different sources, and creating interactive dashboards and reports.

Advanced Charting

Excel offers advanced charting options to create visually appealing and informative charts. You can customize charts extensively to highlight important data points, add labels, and apply various styles.

For advanced charting, explore options like sparklines, trendlines, and error bars, and consider combining multiple chart types in a single chart for comprehensive data representation.

Excel's macros and advanced tools, including VBA, UDFs, add-ins like Solver and Analysis ToolPak, Power Query, Power Pivot, and advanced charting, empower you to automate tasks, extend Excel's capabilities, and perform complex data analysis and modeling. By mastering these advanced features, you can become a more efficient and proficient Excel user.

Chapter 4: PowerPoint Proficiency

4.1. Crafting Compelling Presentations

Creating effective and compelling presentations is a valuable skill in both professional and educational settings. PowerPoint, a part of the Microsoft Office suite, offers a range of tools and features to help you craft visually appealing and impactful presentations. In this section, we will explore the fundamentals of crafting compelling presentations using PowerPoint.

Understanding the Purpose

Before diving into PowerPoint, it's crucial to understand the purpose of your presentation. Ask yourself:

- What message or information do you want to convey?
- Who is your target audience?
- What is the desired outcome of your presentation?

Having a clear understanding of these aspects will guide your content creation and design choices.

Structuring Your Presentation

A well-structured presentation follows a logical flow that keeps the audience engaged. Consider organizing your content into the following sections:

1. **Title Slide**: The first slide typically includes the presentation title, your name, and affiliation.

2. **Agenda or Outline**: Provide an overview of the topics you will cover.

3. **Introduction**: Set the stage by introducing the topic and its significance.

4. **Main Content**: This is where you present the core information, ideas, or data. Use bullet points, visuals, and clear headings for each section.

5. **Visual Aids**: Include relevant images, charts, graphs, and multimedia to support your content.

6. **Summary or Conclusion**: Summarize the key points and restate the main message.

7. **Q&A and Discussion**: Allocate time for questions and open discussion if appropriate.

8. **Closing**: Conclude your presentation with a memorable closing statement or call to action.

Design Principles

The design of your presentation greatly impacts its effectiveness. Here are some design principles to keep in mind:

- **Consistency**: Maintain a consistent look throughout your slides. Use the same fonts, colors, and styles.

- **Simplicity**: Avoid clutter and overly complex visuals. Keep slides clean and uncluttered.

- **Visual Hierarchy**: Emphasize important points using larger fonts, bold text, or colors.

- **Contrast**: Use contrasting colors for text and background to ensure readability.

- **Alignment**: Align elements (text, images, etc.) to create a clean and organized layout.

Text and Typography

Text plays a crucial role in presentations. Use these guidelines for effective text usage:

- Limit the amount of text on each slide. Use bullet points and concise sentences.

- Choose legible fonts like Arial, Calibri, or Helvetica.

- Maintain font size consistency (e.g., use a larger font for slide titles).

- Avoid excessive use of text effects, such as animations or word art.

Visuals and Graphics

Well-chosen visuals enhance the impact of your presentation. Here are some tips:

- Use high-quality images and graphics. Avoid pixelation or distortion.

- Use visuals to complement your message, not distract from it.

- Incorporate charts and graphs to simplify complex data.

- Animate visuals sparingly, and ensure animations are meaningful.

Slide Transitions and Animations

Slide transitions and animations can add flair to your presentation but should be used judiciously:

- Choose slide transitions that suit the tone of your presentation (e.g., subtle fades or slides).

- Use animations to reveal content sequentially, making it easier for the audience to follow.

- Avoid overly flashy transitions or animations that may distract from your message.

Rehearse your presentation multiple times to ensure a smooth delivery:

- Practice speaking clearly and confidently.

- Familiarize yourself with the content so you can speak naturally.

- Time your presentation to stay within your allotted timeframe.

- Be prepared to answer questions or engage in discussions.

Crafting compelling presentations in PowerPoint is both an art and a skill. By understanding your purpose, structuring your content effectively, applying design principles, and utilizing text, visuals, and animations thoughtfully, you can create presentations that engage your audience and effectively convey your message. Practice and rehearsal are essential to delivering presentations with confidence and impact.

4.2. Advanced Design and Layout Techniques

In PowerPoint, advanced design and layout techniques can elevate the visual appeal and professionalism of your presentations. Whether you're creating a business proposal, educational lecture, or a creative pitch, paying attention to design details can make a significant difference. In this section, we will delve into advanced design and layout techniques in PowerPoint.

Master Slides

Master slides are foundational templates that control the overall design of your presentation. They allow you to set the theme, fonts, colors, background styles, and placeholders for your entire presentation. To access and customize master slides:

1. Go to the "View" tab.

2. Click on "Slide Master."

3. Here, you can make global changes that will apply to all slides. Edit fonts, colors, backgrounds, and placeholders to create a consistent look.

Using master slides ensures that your presentation maintains a cohesive and professional appearance throughout.

Custom Slide Layouts

PowerPoint provides standard slide layouts, such as title slides, content slides, and section headers. However, you can create custom slide layouts tailored to your specific content and design requirements:

1. In the "Slide Master" view, select the slide layout you want to customize.

2. Modify the layout by adding placeholders, graphics, or any other elements.

3. Save the custom layout, and it will be available for use in your presentation.

Creating custom slide layouts gives you more control over how your content is presented and helps maintain consistency.

SmartArt Graphics

SmartArt graphics in PowerPoint allow you to visually represent processes, hierarchies, lists, and more. They provide a dynamic and engaging way to convey complex information. To insert SmartArt graphics:

1. Go to the "Insert" tab.

2. Click on "SmartArt."

3. Choose a SmartArt graphic that suits your content.

4. Enter your text into the SmartArt shapes, and they will automatically adjust to fit.

Customize the colors, styles, and arrangement of your SmartArt graphic to match your presentation's design.

Object Alignment and Distribution

Precise alignment and distribution of objects on a slide can greatly enhance its visual appeal. Use PowerPoint's alignment and distribution tools to achieve this:

- **Align**: Select multiple objects, right-click, and choose "Align" to align them horizontally or vertically.

- **Distribute**: Similarly, select objects, right-click, and choose "Distribute" to evenly space them horizontally or vertically.

These tools help maintain a clean and organized layout, especially when working with complex slide designs.

Design Themes and Variants

PowerPoint offers design themes and variants that provide a quick way to change the overall look and feel of your presentation:

1. Go to the "Design" tab.

2. Browse through the design themes and variants available.

3. Click on a theme or variant to apply it to your presentation.

Design themes and variants can instantly transform the appearance of your slides while maintaining consistency.

Custom Animation and Transitions

To add engaging animations and transitions to your slides:

- Select a slide element (e.g., text box or image).

- Go to the "Animations" tab to choose from various animation effects.

- Use the "Transition" tab to apply slide transitions between different slides.

While animations and transitions can enhance your presentation, use them judiciously to avoid overwhelming your audience.

Slide Show Customization

Customizing the slide show settings can improve the audience's viewing experience:

- Go to the "Slide Show" tab.

- Use options like "Presenter View" to see speaker notes, "Slide Show Monitor" to choose the display, and "Custom Slide Show" to create a specific sequence of slides.

Custom slide show settings allow you to tailor the presentation for different scenarios.

Mastering advanced design and layout techniques in PowerPoint empowers you to create presentations that are not only visually appealing but also effectively convey your message. By utilizing master slides, custom layouts, SmartArt graphics, object alignment, design themes, animations, and transitions thoughtfully, you can create impactful presentations tailored to your audience and purpose.

4.3. Incorporating Multimedia Elements

Multimedia elements, such as images, videos, and audio, can enhance the richness and engagement of your PowerPoint presentations. In this section, we'll explore how to effectively incorporate multimedia elements into your slides.

Inserting Images

Images are a powerful way to convey information and add visual appeal to your presentation. To insert images into your slides:

1. Go to the slide where you want to add the image.

2. Click on the "Insert" tab.

3. Choose "Pictures" to select an image file from your computer or "Online Pictures" to search for images online.

4. Once inserted, you can resize, move, and format the image as needed.

When using images, ensure they are relevant to your content and high-quality to maintain professionalism.

Working with Graphics

In addition to images, PowerPoint provides various graphic elements that can enhance your slides:

- **Shapes**: Use shapes to create diagrams, callout boxes, or custom design elements. You can customize their colors, sizes, and styles.

- **Icons**: PowerPoint offers a library of icons that you can easily insert and customize to represent concepts or actions.

- **SmartArt**: SmartArt graphics can be used to illustrate processes, hierarchies, and relationships in a visually appealing way.

These graphic elements can be found in the "Insert" tab and allow you to create custom visual content.

Embedding Videos

Embedding videos into your PowerPoint presentation can make it more dynamic and engaging. Follow these steps to insert a video:

1. Go to the slide where you want to add the video.

2. Click on the "Insert" tab.

3. Choose "Video" and select either "Online Video" to embed a video from the web or "Video on My PC" to insert a video file from your computer.

4. Adjust the video size and position on the slide.

5. You can also set video playback options, such as automatic playback or looping.

Ensure that your video file format is compatible with PowerPoint to avoid playback issues.

Adding Audio

Including audio, such as narration or background music, can enhance the multimedia experience of your presentation. Here's how to add audio:

1. Go to the slide where you want to add audio.

2. Click on the "Insert" tab.

3. Choose "Audio" and select either "Audio on My PC" to insert an audio file or "Online Audio" to search for audio clips online.

4. Customize the audio playback options, such as starting automatically or looping.

Audio can be useful for providing additional context or guiding the audience through your presentation.

Managing Multimedia

To manage multimedia elements efficiently:

- Use the "Selection Pane" in the "Home" tab to control the visibility and stacking order of objects on your slide.

- Ensure that multimedia elements don't overpower your content; they should complement your message.

- Test multimedia elements before your actual presentation to ensure they work correctly.

- Keep multimedia files organized in a dedicated folder to prevent broken links.

Compressing Media

If your presentation contains many multimedia elements and becomes large in file size, consider compressing media to make it more manageable:

1. Go to the "File" tab.

2. Select "Info."

3. Click on "Compress Media" to reduce the size of images and videos in your presentation.

Compressing media can help your presentation load faster and be more easily shared.

Linked vs. Embedded Media

When inserting multimedia elements, you have the option to either link or embed them:

- **Linked Media**: Linked media references external files. This can keep your presentation file size smaller but requires the linked files to be available when presenting.

- **Embedded Media**: Embedded media is stored within the presentation file. It makes the file larger but ensures that the multimedia elements are self-contained.

Choose the option that best suits your needs, considering factors like file size and portability.

Incorporating multimedia elements into your PowerPoint presentations allows you to create engaging and informative content. By using images, graphics, videos, and audio strategically, you can enhance your message and captivate your audience. Remember to manage multimedia elements effectively and consider compressing media to optimize your presentation's performance.

4.4. Presentation Tips and Tricks

Creating an effective PowerPoint presentation involves more than just design and content. It also requires careful planning, structure, and delivery. In this section, we will explore some valuable tips and tricks to help you deliver engaging and impactful presentations.

Storytelling Techniques

PowerPoint presentations often tell a story, whether it's a narrative about a project, a sales pitch, or an educational lecture. To engage your audience, consider the following storytelling techniques:

- **Start with a Hook**: Begin your presentation with an attention-grabbing hook or anecdote to pique your audience's interest.

- **Structure with a Narrative Arc**: Organize your content using a narrative arc, including an introduction, rising action, climax, falling action, and resolution.

- **Use Visuals**: Visuals, such as images and diagrams, can help convey your story more effectively than text alone.

- **Provide Examples and Scenarios**: Real-life examples and scenarios make your content relatable and memorable.

Slide Content and Design

Effective slide content and design are crucial for audience engagement:

- **Limit Text**: Avoid overcrowded slides with too much text. Use concise bullet points and visuals to convey your message.

- **Font Size**: Ensure that text is easily readable. Use a larger font size for slide titles and a smaller size for content.

- **Consistency**: Maintain a consistent design throughout your presentation. Use the same fonts, colors, and slide layouts.

- **Whitespace**: Utilize whitespace to create clean and uncluttered slides. It improves readability and aesthetics.

Slide Transitions and Animations

While transitions and animations can enhance your presentation, they should be used thoughtfully:

- **Transitions**: Choose subtle slide transitions that match the tone of your presentation. Avoid distracting transitions.

- **Animations**: Use animations to reveal content sequentially, making it easier for the audience to follow. Avoid excessive or flashy animations.

Practice and Rehearsal

Practice and rehearsal are essential for a smooth presentation:

- **Practice**: Practice your presentation multiple times to become comfortable with the content and flow.

- **Timing**: Time your presentation to ensure it fits within the allotted timeframe. Adjust as needed.

- **Rehearse with Feedback**: If possible, rehearse in front of a trusted colleague or friend who can provide feedback.

Audience Engagement

Engaging your audience keeps them attentive and interested:

- **Interactivity**: Incorporate interactive elements, such as questions, polls, or discussions, to involve the audience.

- **Eye Contact**: Maintain eye contact with the audience to establish a connection and convey confidence.

- **Body Language**: Use open and confident body language. Avoid nervous habits like fidgeting.

Backup Plans

Prepare for unexpected situations:

- **Backup Files**: Have backup copies of your presentation on a USB drive or in the cloud.

- **Test Equipment**: Arrive early to test the presentation equipment and ensure everything works correctly.

Be prepared to handle questions effectively:

- **Q&A Session**: Allocate time for questions at the end of your presentation or after each section, depending on your preference.

- **Anticipate Questions**: Consider potential questions your audience might ask and have answers ready.

- **Stay Calm**: If you don't know the answer to a question, stay calm and offer to follow up later with the information.

Closing Strong

End your presentation on a memorable note:

- **Summary**: Summarize the key points to reinforce your message.

- **Call to Action**: If applicable, provide a clear call to action or next steps for the audience.

Thank

4.5. Sharing and Collaborating on Presentations

Sharing and collaborating on PowerPoint presentations is essential for team projects, remote work, and knowledge sharing. Microsoft Office provides various tools and features to facilitate collaboration and sharing. In this section, we'll explore how to effectively share and collaborate on your PowerPoint presentations.

1. Share Online

One of the easiest ways to collaborate on a presentation is by sharing it online using OneDrive or SharePoint. Here's how:

- Save your presentation on OneDrive or SharePoint.

- Click the "Share" button in PowerPoint.

- Enter the email addresses of collaborators, choose their permission level (e.g., view, edit), and send invitations.

- Collaborators can access the presentation via a web browser and edit it in real-time.

2. Co-Authoring

Co-authoring allows multiple users to work on the same PowerPoint presentation simultaneously. It's available when the presentation is stored on OneDrive or SharePoint. Here's how to use it:

- Open the presentation in PowerPoint Online.

- Click the "Edit in Browser" button.

- Collaborators can join the presentation and edit it together in real-time. Changes are automatically saved.

3. Comments and Review

To facilitate feedback and review, you can use the commenting feature in PowerPoint:

- Select the slide or element you want to comment on.

- Click the "Review" tab and then "New Comment."

- Enter your comment, and it will be associated with the selected content.

- Collaborators can reply to comments, making it easy to discuss changes and improvements.

4. Version History

PowerPoint keeps a version history of your presentation, allowing you to revert to previous versions if needed. To access version history:

- Go to OneDrive or SharePoint.

- Right-click on the presentation file and choose "Version History."

- Review and restore previous versions if necessary.

5. Password Protection

If you want to restrict access to your presentation, you can password-protect it:

- Click the "File" tab, select "Info," and then "Protect Presentation."

- Choose "Encrypt with Password" and enter a password.

- Share the password only with authorized collaborators.

6. Export and Sharing Options

PowerPoint provides various export and sharing options:

- Export your presentation as a PDF, which ensures that the formatting remains consistent.

- Use the "Embed" option to generate an HTML code that you can embed in a website or blog.

- Share your presentation as a link via email or social media.

7. Offline Collaboration

If you need to collaborate on a PowerPoint presentation offline, you can use the "Track Changes" feature:

- Click the "Review" tab and enable "Track Changes."

- Make your edits, and PowerPoint will track them with colored highlights and comments.

- Collaborators can review and accept/reject changes when they have access to the file.

8. Sharing with External Users

If you need to share your presentation with external users who don't have Microsoft accounts, you can generate a guest link:

- Click the "Share" button in PowerPoint.

- Select "Create Guest Link" and set the permissions.

- Share the generated link with external users, and they can view or edit the presentation without signing in.

9. Offline File Sharing

For situations where internet access is limited, you can share PowerPoint files offline using USB drives, email attachments, or cloud storage providers that offer offline synchronization.

10. Feedback and Collaboration Tools

Consider using additional collaboration tools, such as Microsoft Teams, Slack, or project management software, to streamline communication and collaboration on PowerPoint presentations.

Effective sharing and collaboration on PowerPoint presentations are crucial for productivity and teamwork. By leveraging the features and tools provided by Microsoft Office, you can work seamlessly with colleagues, clients, or partners, whether you're in the same office or collaborating remotely. Remember to set permissions and access levels appropriately to ensure the security and integrity of your presentation.

Chapter 5: Outlook Optimization

5.1. Email Management and Organization

Email is a fundamental tool for communication and productivity in today's professional world. Microsoft Outlook offers a robust set of features for managing and organizing your emails effectively. In this section, we will explore various strategies and techniques to optimize your email management and organization in Outlook.

1. Inbox Organization

1.1. Focusing on the Inbox Zero Concept

The Inbox Zero concept encourages keeping your inbox empty or nearly empty by processing emails promptly. When you receive an email, you can:

- **Delete**: If the email is irrelevant or spam, delete it.

- **Archive**: If the email contains important information but doesn't require immediate action, archive it.

- **Reply or Delegate**: If you can respond in a few minutes, do so. If the email is a task for someone else, delegate it.

- **Flag or Label**: Flag or label emails that need your attention but can't be addressed immediately.

- **Move to Folders**: Use folders to categorize and organize emails. Create folders for specific projects, clients, or topics.

1.2. Use Rules and Filters

Outlook allows you to create rules and filters to automate email organization. For example:

- Automatically move emails from specific senders to designated folders.

- Apply labels or categories to incoming emails based on keywords or sender addresses.

2. Email Prioritization

2.1. Flagging and Categorizing

Flag important emails for follow-up by setting due dates. Categorize emails with colors or labels to indicate their importance or context.

2.2. Focused Inbox

Outlook's Focused Inbox separates important emails from less important ones. It learns from your behavior and helps you focus on the emails that matter most.

3. Email Search

Outlook offers powerful search capabilities to find specific emails quickly:

- Use keywords, sender names, or dates in the search bar.
- Use advanced search operators to refine your search.

4. Email Templates

If you frequently send similar emails, create templates to save time. Outlook allows you to save email drafts as templates for reuse.

5. Email Signatures

Customize your email signature with your contact information, job title, and branding elements. Outlook allows you to create multiple signatures for different purposes.

6. Email Cleanup

6.1. *Clutter Folder*

Outlook's Clutter feature automatically moves low-priority emails to a designated Clutter folder. Review the Clutter folder periodically to ensure important emails aren't missed.

6.2. *Sweep and Archive*

Use the "Sweep" feature to clean up your inbox by moving or deleting emails from a particular sender or category. Archive older emails to keep your inbox clutter-free.

7. Email Security and Privacy

7.1. *Spam Filters and Junk Email*

Outlook's spam filters help reduce unwanted emails. Regularly check your Junk Email folder to make sure legitimate emails aren't marked as spam.

7.2. *Phishing Protection*

Be cautious of phishing emails and suspicious links. Outlook includes built-in phishing protection, but always verify the sender's authenticity.

8. Email Management on Mobile Devices

Outlook is available on various mobile platforms. Sync your emails and calendar to stay productive while on the go. Use mobile-friendly features like swipe gestures for quick actions.

9. Email Signature Management

If you use Outlook on multiple devices, ensure that your email signature is consistent across all platforms. Outlook can sync your signature settings.

10. Backup and Data Recovery

Regularly back up your Outlook data to prevent data loss. Microsoft provides tools for exporting and importing email data, ensuring you can recover essential emails if needed.

By implementing these strategies and techniques, you can optimize your email management and organization in Microsoft Outlook. Whether you're dealing with a high volume of emails, working on important projects, or striving for a clutter-free inbox, Outlook's features and best practices can help you stay productive and organized in your email communication.

5.2. Calendar and Scheduling Mastery

Managing your calendar effectively is essential for staying organized and ensuring you make the most of your time. Microsoft Outlook provides powerful calendar and scheduling features that help you keep track of appointments, meetings, and events. In this section, we will delve into mastering your calendar and scheduling in Outlook.

1. Creating Events and Appointments

1.1. *Creating Appointments*

Appointments in Outlook are personal time blocks without attendees. To create an appointment:

- Click on the "Calendar" icon in the navigation pane.
- Select the date and time for your appointment.
- Enter a subject, location, and any additional details.
- Set reminders to receive notifications.
- Click "Save & Close."

1.2. *Creating Events*

Events in Outlook often involve inviting others to meetings or activities. To create an event:

- Click on the "Calendar" icon in the navigation pane.
- Select the date and time for your event.
- Enter a subject, location, and any necessary details.
- Click on the "Invite Attendees" button to add participants from your contacts or directory.

- Set reminders and choose whether to receive responses.
- Click "Send" to invite attendees.

2. Scheduling Meetings

Outlook simplifies scheduling meetings with its integrated scheduling assistant:

- Start creating a new event or appointment.
- Add attendees by typing their names or email addresses in the "Attendees" field.
- Click on the "Scheduling Assistant" to view attendees' availability.
- Choose a suitable time slot when all attendees are available.
- Outlook automatically sends invitations to attendees with the meeting details.

3. Setting Recurring Appointments and Meetings

For recurring events, appointments, or meetings:

- While creating an event or appointment, click on the "Recurrence" button.
- Specify the recurrence pattern (daily, weekly, monthly, etc.) and details.
- Define the end date or number of occurrences.
- Outlook will generate recurring instances on your calendar.

4. Customizing Calendar Views

Outlook offers various calendar views, including day, week, month, and year views. You can also create custom views:

- Click on the "View" tab in the calendar.
- Select a view or click "Change View" to create a custom view.
- Customize the view by selecting which calendars to display, changing the time scale, or adding additional details.

5. Color-Coding and Categorizing

Use color-coding and categories to visually distinguish between different types of appointments and events:

- Right-click on an appointment or event and choose "Categorize."
- Assign a category and choose a color.
- Now, your calendar items will be color-coded for easy identification.

6. Sharing Calendars

Outlook allows you to share your calendar with colleagues or friends:

- Right-click on your calendar in the navigation pane.
- Select "Share" and choose the permissions you want to grant (view, edit).
- Enter the email addresses of the recipients.
- They will receive invitations to access your calendar.

7. Accepting and Declining Invitations

When you receive meeting invitations:

- Open the email invitation, and click "Accept," "Tentative," or "Decline."
- The event is automatically added to your calendar.
- You can also propose a new time if the suggested time doesn't work.

8. Meeting Responses

As a meeting organizer, you can track attendees' responses:

- Open the event on your calendar.
- Click the "Tracking" tab to see who has accepted, declined, or not responded to the invitation.

9. Adding Holidays and Birthdays

You can add holidays and birthdays to your calendar for reference:

- Click on "File" and select "Options."
- In the "Calendar" section, click "Add Holidays" or "Add Birthday Calendar."
- Follow the prompts to add the desired events.

10. Mobile Calendar Sync

Sync your Outlook calendar with your mobile device to stay updated on the go:

- Install the Outlook app on your mobile device.
- Sign in with your Outlook account.
- Your calendar will automatically sync, allowing you to access and manage your events from anywhere.

Mastering your calendar and scheduling in Outlook streamlines your daily routines, ensures you never miss an important appointment, and enhances your overall productivity. Whether you're setting up one-time events, recurring meetings, or collaborating with colleagues, Outlook's versatile features empower you to manage your time effectively.

5.3. Contacts and Task Management

Microsoft Outlook offers robust tools for managing your contacts and tasks, helping you stay organized and efficient in your professional and personal life. In this section, we will explore how to effectively manage contacts and tasks within Outlook.

Contacts Management

Outlook's contacts feature allows you to store and organize information about people and organizations you interact with. Here's how to effectively manage your contacts:

1. **Adding Contacts**: To add a new contact, click on the "People" icon in the navigation pane and then click "New Contact." Enter the contact's details, including name, email, phone number, address, and additional notes.

2. **Categorizing Contacts**: You can categorize contacts using labels or categories. This helps in grouping and quickly finding specific contacts. Right-click on a contact, choose "Categorize," and select a category.

3. **Contact Groups**: Create contact groups (formerly known as distribution lists) for sending emails or invitations to multiple contacts simultaneously. Click "New Contact Group" and add members from your contacts.

4. **Contact Photos**: Add photos to contacts to make them easily recognizable. Open a contact, click on the default image, and upload a photo.

5. **Importing and Exporting Contacts**: If you have contacts in other applications or formats, you can import them into Outlook. To export contacts, select them, click "File," and choose "Export."

6. **Contact Sharing**: You can share your contacts with others in your organization. Right-click on a contact folder, select "Share," and set permissions.

7. **Contact Search**: Use the search bar in the People view to quickly find specific contacts. You can search by name, email address, or other details.

Task Management

Outlook's task feature helps you track and manage your to-do lists and projects efficiently. Here's how to effectively manage your tasks:

1. **Creating Tasks**: To create a new task, click on the "Tasks" icon in the navigation pane and then click "New Task." Enter the task's subject, due date, priority, and additional notes.

2. **Task Categories**: Similar to contacts, you can categorize tasks using labels or categories. Right-click on a task, choose "Categorize," and select a category.

3. **Task Assignments**: If you work in a team, you can assign tasks to colleagues. Open a task, click "Assign Task," and enter the assignee's email address.

4. **Task Status**: Tasks can have different statuses such as "Not Started," "In Progress," and "Completed." You can mark tasks as complete, and they will move to the "Completed Tasks" folder.

5. **Task Due Dates and Reminders**: Set due dates and reminders for tasks to stay on top of your commitments. Outlook will notify you when a task is due.

6. **Task Recurrence**: For recurring tasks, you can set up daily, weekly, monthly, or custom recurrence patterns.

7. **Task Attachments**: Attach files or emails to tasks for reference or additional information.

8. **Task Views**: Customize your task views by selecting different arrangements and sorting options. Use the "To-Do List" view for a quick overview of pending tasks.

9. **Task Sharing**: You can share task lists with others to collaborate on projects. Right-click on a task folder, select "Share," and set permissions.

10. **Task Search**: Use the search bar in the Tasks view to quickly find specific tasks. You can search by subject, due date, or other details.

11. **Flagged Emails as Tasks**: You can convert emails into tasks by right-clicking on an email and selecting "Add to Tasks" or "Flag for Follow-Up."

12. **Task Prioritization**: Assign priority levels to tasks to help you focus on what needs to be done first.

Integration with Calendar

Outlook integrates tasks and appointments, allowing you to schedule tasks directly in your calendar. This helps you allocate time for specific tasks and ensure they are completed on schedule.

Mobile Task Management

Sync your Outlook tasks with your mobile device to access and manage them on the go using the Outlook mobile app. This ensures you stay productive even when you're not at your desk.

Effective contacts and task management in Outlook are essential for maintaining productivity and organization in your daily life. Whether you're managing a contact list, collaborating on projects, or keeping track of personal tasks, Outlook's features and best practices empower you to stay on top of your commitments and responsibilities.

5.4. Using Outlook for Effective Communication

Microsoft Outlook is not just an email client; it's a powerful communication tool that allows you to manage your emails, calendar, contacts, and more. In this section, we'll explore how to use Outlook for effective communication, whether you're sending emails, scheduling meetings, or collaborating with colleagues.

1. Email Communication

Outlook's primary function is email management. Here are some tips for effective email communication:

- **Clear and Concise Emails**: Write clear and concise email messages. Start with a brief, informative subject line and use paragraphs for readability.

- **Professional Email Signature**: Create a professional email signature that includes your name, title, organization, and contact information. Outlook allows you to set up multiple signatures for different purposes.

- **Reply and Forward with Care**: When replying to or forwarding emails, review the entire thread to ensure you provide context and avoid confusion.

- **Attachments**: When sending attachments, make sure they are relevant and necessary. Compress large files to reduce email size.

- **Use BCC for Privacy**: When sending emails to multiple recipients who don't need to know each other's email addresses, use the "BCC" (blind carbon copy) field to protect their privacy.

- **Use Read Receipts Sparingly**: Avoid requesting read receipts for every email, as it can be perceived as invasive. Reserve read receipts for important or time-sensitive messages.

2. Calendar and Meeting Management

Outlook's calendar and meeting features help you schedule and manage appointments and meetings efficiently:

- **Meeting Requests**: When scheduling meetings, use Outlook's "Meeting Request" feature. This allows you to invite attendees, set a date and time, and track responses.

- **Responding to Meeting Requests**: Respond promptly to meeting invitations, whether you accept, decline, or propose a new time. This helps organizers plan effectively.

- **Meeting Reminders**: Set reminders for meetings and appointments to ensure you don't forget important commitments.

- **Share Your Calendar**: Share your calendar with colleagues to facilitate scheduling and avoid conflicts. Outlook allows you to specify the level of detail others can see.

3. Contact Management

Outlook's contact management features help you keep track of important contacts:

- **Complete Contact Information**: Ensure your contacts have complete and up-to-date information, including email addresses, phone numbers, and job titles.

- **Contact Groups**: Create contact groups for sending emails or meeting invitations to multiple contacts simultaneously.

- **Contact Sharing**: Share contact lists with colleagues to streamline communication and collaboration.

4. Email Etiquette

Effective communication in Outlook also involves email etiquette:

- **Use a Professional Tone**: Maintain a professional and courteous tone in your emails, whether you're communicating with colleagues, clients, or superiors.

- **Avoid Overuse of Capitalization and Exclamation Marks**: Using excessive capitalization or exclamation marks can come across as shouting. Use them sparingly for emphasis.

- **Respect Working Hours**: Be mindful of time zones and working hours when scheduling meetings or sending emails to colleagues in different locations.

- **Use Out of Office Messages**: Set up an out-of-office message when you're away to inform senders of your unavailability and provide an alternative contact if necessary.

- **Avoid Overloading with Information**: Keep emails concise and focused on one topic. If you need to discuss multiple subjects, consider sending separate emails.

- **Proofread and Spell Check**: Proofread your emails and use the built-in spell check feature to avoid typos and grammatical errors.

5. Mobile Communication

Outlook is available on mobile devices, allowing you to stay connected and productive while on the go. Install the Outlook app on your smartphone or tablet to access your emails, calendar, and contacts from anywhere.

6. Integrating Communication Tools

Outlook integrates with other Microsoft 365 tools like Teams and OneDrive, enabling seamless communication and collaboration. You can schedule Teams meetings directly from Outlook and share files stored in OneDrive.

Effective communication in Outlook enhances your productivity and ensures that you stay organized in a fast-paced work environment. Whether you're managing emails, scheduling meetings, or maintaining contact lists, using Outlook's features and adhering to communication best practices can significantly improve your professional communication.

5.5. Customizing Outlook for Personal Productivity

Customization is a key aspect of getting the most out of Microsoft Outlook for your personal productivity. Outlook offers a wide range of customization options that allow you to tailor the application to your specific needs and preferences. In this section, we will explore how you can customize Outlook to boost your personal productivity.

1. Customize the Ribbon

The Ribbon is the toolbar at the top of the Outlook window that contains various tabs and commands. You can customize it to include the commands you use most frequently:

- Right-click on the Ribbon and select "Customize the Ribbon."
- Create custom tabs and groups and add commands to them.
- Rearrange or remove tabs and groups to streamline your workflow.

2. Quick Access Toolbar

The Quick Access Toolbar is a small toolbar located above the Ribbon. You can customize it by adding commands you frequently use:

- Click on the drop-down arrow on the Quick Access Toolbar.
- Select the commands you want to add from the list.
- You can also move it below the Ribbon for better visibility.

3. Email Signatures

Create and customize email signatures that can include your name, title, contact information, and even images or logos:

- Go to "File" > "Options" > "Mail."

- In the "Compose messages" section, click on "Signatures."

- Create, edit, or delete signatures and set default signatures for new emails and replies.

4. Views and Layouts

Customize the way you view your emails, calendar, and other Outlook items:

- Adjust the reading pane position, size, and whether it's shown or hidden.

- Customize the layout of your emails by choosing how message previews are displayed.

- In the Calendar, choose the day and time slot format that suits your needs.

5. Rules and Alerts

Outlook's Rules and Alerts feature allows you to automate actions based on specific criteria. This can help you manage your inbox more efficiently:

- Create rules to automatically move, categorize, or flag emails.

- Set up alerts for specific keywords, senders, or subjects.

- Create custom rules to sort your emails as they arrive.

6. Quick Steps

Quick Steps in Outlook are one-click actions that you can customize for common tasks:

- Create custom Quick Steps to move emails to specific folders, forward messages to colleagues, or perform other actions with a single click.

- You can also edit or delete existing Quick Steps to fit your workflow.

7. Keyboard Shortcuts

Learn and use keyboard shortcuts to navigate Outlook more efficiently:

- Press "Ctrl + /" to open the search box.

- Use "Ctrl + N" to start a new email.

- "Ctrl + Enter" sends an email.

- Customize keyboard shortcuts to your liking by going to "File" > "Options" > "Quick Access Toolbar."

8. Themes and Colors

Customize the appearance of Outlook with different themes and color schemes:

- Go to "File" > "Options" > "General."

- Choose your desired Office theme (e.g., Dark Gray, Light Gray, Black) and customize your Office background.

9. Advanced Settings

Explore advanced settings in Outlook to fine-tune your experience:

- Adjust email delivery options, including the frequency of email checking.

- Customize the AutoArchive settings to manage your email storage efficiently.

- Configure data file settings to manage your mailbox size.

10. Add-Ins and Extensions

Explore Outlook add-ins and extensions available in the Microsoft Office Store:

- Add-ins can extend Outlook's functionality, such as integrating with project management tools, CRM systems, or email tracking solutions.

- Install and customize add-ins that align with your workflow and productivity goals.

Customizing Outlook to match your preferences and workflow can significantly enhance your productivity. Whether it's simplifying common tasks, streamlining email management, or optimizing the user interface, Outlook's customization options empower you to create an email and productivity tool that works best for you.

Chapter 6: Access and Database Management

Section 6.1: Introduction to Database Concepts

In this section, we will delve into the fundamental concepts of databases and their significance in the realm of Microsoft Access. Databases are powerful tools for organizing and managing data efficiently. Whether you are tracking customer information, managing inventory, or analyzing sales data, understanding database concepts is essential for making the most of Microsoft Access.

What is a Database?

A **database** is a structured collection of data organized in a way that allows for efficient storage, retrieval, and manipulation. Think of it as a digital filing cabinet where you can store and retrieve information quickly. Databases are designed to handle large volumes of data and provide a structured framework for organizing it.

Key Database Terminology

Before diving deeper into Access, let's familiarize ourselves with some key database terminology:

1. **Table:** A table is a fundamental component of a database. It represents a collection of related data organized into rows (records) and columns (fields). Each row in a table represents a single entity or record, and each column represents a specific attribute or piece of information.

2. **Record:** A record is a single row in a table that contains all the data related to a specific entity. For example, in a customer database, each record might represent one customer's information.

3. **Field:** A field is a column in a table that stores a specific type of data, such as names, addresses, or dates. Fields define the type of information that can be stored in a table.

4. **Primary Key:** A primary key is a unique identifier for each record in a table. It ensures that each record can be uniquely identified and retrieved. In many cases, a primary key is an auto-incrementing number.

5. **Relationship:** Relationships define how different tables are related to each other. For example, in a database for a library, there might be a relationship between the "Books" table and the "Authors" table, linking books to their respective authors.

6. **Query:** A query is a request for specific information from a database. It allows you to filter, sort, and extract data based on certain criteria.

Why Use Databases?

Databases offer several advantages over traditional data storage methods like spreadsheets or text files:

- **Data Integrity:** Databases enforce rules and constraints that help maintain data accuracy and consistency.

- **Efficient Retrieval:** Databases allow for quick and precise retrieval of data, even from large datasets.

- **Scalability:** Databases can handle large volumes of data and can grow with your needs.

- **Security:** Databases provide access control and security features to protect sensitive data.

- **Multi-User Support:** Many databases, including Access, support multiple users simultaneously, allowing for collaborative data management.

In the upcoming sections of this chapter, we will explore how to create and work with databases in Microsoft Access, design tables, establish relationships between them, and perform queries to extract meaningful information. Understanding these database concepts is foundational to becoming proficient in Access.

Section 6.2: Building and Designing Databases in Access

Now that we've established a foundation of database concepts in Section 6.1, let's dive into the practical aspects of building and designing databases using Microsoft Access. Microsoft Access is a user-friendly database management system that allows you to create, maintain, and manipulate databases with ease. In this section, we'll explore the steps involved in creating a database and designing its structure.

Creating a New Database

1. **Launch Microsoft Access:** Start by opening Microsoft Access on your computer. You can typically find it in the Microsoft Office suite.

2. **Choose a Database Template (Optional):** Access offers a variety of database templates for common purposes like inventory management, contacts, or project tracking. You can select a template that closely matches your needs, or you can start with a blank database for full customization.

3. **Define the Database Name and Location:** Give your database a meaningful name and specify where you want to save it on your computer or a network location.

4. **Create Tables:** Tables are the foundation of any database. They hold your data and define its structure. You can create tables from scratch or use predefined templates if you started with one.

Designing Tables

Designing tables is a critical aspect of creating a well-structured database. Here are key considerations when designing tables in Access:

Field Names and Data Types

- **Field Names:** Choose descriptive and concise names for each field (column) in your table. For example, in a "Customers" table, you might have fields like "CustomerID," "FirstName," "LastName," and "Email."

- **Data Types:** Access provides various data types for fields, such as Text, Number, Date/Time, and Currency. Select the appropriate data type for each field to ensure data accuracy and efficient storage.

- **Primary Key:** Every table should have a primary key, a unique identifier for each record. Access often suggests an auto-incrementing number field as the primary key. It ensures that each record is unique and can be retrieved efficiently.

- **Relationships:** If your database involves multiple tables, establish relationships between them to connect related data. For example, if you have a "Customers" table and an "Orders" table, you can create a relationship based on the "CustomerID" field to associate each order with a customer.

- **Validation Rules:** Define validation rules to ensure data integrity. For instance, you can set a validation rule for a "Phone Number" field to accept only valid phone numbers.

- **Validation Text:** Provide clear validation text that explains the rules to users when they enter data that doesn't meet validation criteria.

Creating Forms, Queries, and Reports

Once your tables are designed, you can use Access to create:

- **Forms:** Forms allow users to enter and view data in a user-friendly interface. You can design custom forms to match your database's needs.

- **Queries:** Queries help you retrieve specific data from your tables. You can create queries to filter, sort, and analyze your data.

- **Reports:** Reports are used for presenting data in a structured and visually appealing format. You can design reports to generate printed or digital summaries of your database information.

In the following sections of this chapter, we'll explore these aspects in more detail, guiding you through the process of building and designing databases in Microsoft Access. Understanding the principles of table design and relationships is crucial for creating a database that efficiently stores and retrieves your data.

Section 6.3: Querying and Reporting Data

In this section, we will explore the power of querying and reporting data in Microsoft Access. Once you've designed your database and populated it with information, the ability to extract meaningful insights and present data in an organized manner becomes essential. Access provides tools for creating queries to filter and analyze data, as well as for generating reports to present data in a visually appealing format.

Creating Queries

Queries in Access allow you to ask specific questions about your data and retrieve the answers. Here are some key concepts related to creating queries:

Query Design View

- **Query Design View:** To create a query, open your database in Access and navigate to the "Query Design" view. Here, you can define the criteria and layout of your query.

Selecting Fields

- **Selecting Fields:** In your query, you specify which fields (columns) from your tables you want to include in the results. You can choose fields from one or more tables.

Criteria and Filtering

- **Criteria and Filtering:** To narrow down the results, you can set criteria for fields. For example, you can create a query to find all customers who made a purchase in the last month by specifying a date range in the "Order Date" field.

Sorting and Grouping

- **Sorting and Grouping:** Queries can also sort the results based on specific fields and group records with similar values together. For instance, you can create a query to list all products in alphabetical order or group sales by region.

Aggregate Functions

- **Aggregate Functions:** Access supports various aggregate functions like SUM, AVG, COUNT, MIN, and MAX. These functions allow you to perform calculations on data in your query results. For example, you can calculate the total sales amount or the average rating of products.

Parameter Queries

- **Parameter Queries:** Access lets you create parameter queries where users are prompted to enter values when running the query. This makes queries more flexible and user-friendly.

Generating Reports

Reports in Access are used to present data in a structured and visually appealing format. Here are important aspects of report creation:

Report Design View

- **Report Design View:** To create a report, navigate to the "Report Design" view. Here, you can design the layout of your report, including headers, footers, and data sections.

- **Adding Fields:** Like queries, you can specify which fields from your tables to include in the report. You can also add calculated fields based on your data.

- **Formatting and Styling:** Access provides tools for formatting text, numbers, and other elements in your report. You can apply fonts, colors, and styles to make your report visually appealing.

- **Grouping and Sorting:** Reports can group data based on specific fields and sort records within those groups. This is useful for creating summary reports.

- **Page Layout:** You can customize the page layout of your report, including page size, orientation (portrait or landscape), margins, and page numbering.

Exporting and Printing

Access allows you to export reports in various formats, including PDF, Excel, and Word, making it easy to share data with others. You can also print reports directly from the application for physical distribution.

In the upcoming sections of this chapter, we will walk through the process of creating queries and reports in Access. These tools are invaluable for extracting insights from your database and presenting data in a format that is meaningful and understandable to others.

Section 6.4: Access Automation and Customization

Microsoft Access offers a range of automation and customization features that empower users to streamline their database management tasks and adapt the application to their specific needs. In this section, we will delve into the tools and techniques available for automating repetitive tasks and customizing Access to enhance your database workflow.

Macros and Automation

1. **Introduction to Macros:** *Macros are sets of actions that can be recorded and played back in Access. They are incredibly useful for automating repetitive tasks, such as running a series of queries, opening specific forms, or performing data import/export operations.*

2. **Creating Macros:** *You can create macros using the built-in Macro Designer in Access. This interface allows you to add actions, conditions, and loops to your macros, making them capable of responding to specific events or conditions in your database.*

3. **Running Macros:** *Once you've created a macro, you can run it with a single click. Macros can be triggered by various events, including database startup, button clicks, or data changes, offering flexibility in how you automate tasks.*

4. **Automation Examples:** *Common automation tasks include automatically sending email notifications, updating records based on certain criteria, or generating reports on a schedule.*

Visual Basic for Applications (VBA)

5. **Introduction to VBA:** *For advanced automation and customization, Microsoft Access includes a powerful scripting language called Visual Basic for Applications (VBA). VBA allows you to write custom code to control nearly every aspect of Access.*

6. **VBA Code Modules:** *You can create VBA code modules within your database to store and organize your scripts. These modules can contain functions, subroutines, and event handlers.*

7. **Event-Driven Programming:** *VBA in Access is often used for event-driven programming, where code responds to events like button clicks, form openings, or data changes. This makes it possible to create dynamic and interactive database applications.*

8. **Custom Functions:** *With VBA, you can define custom functions that extend the functionality of Access. These functions can perform complex calculations, data manipulations, or interact with external systems.*

9. **Accessing External Data:** *VBA allows you to connect to external data sources, such as Excel, SQL Server, or web services, enabling you to import, export, and manipulate data across various platforms.*

Customizing the Ribbon

10. **Ribbon Customization:** *Access allows you to customize the Ribbon, the toolbar at the top of the application. You can add custom tabs, groups, and buttons to the Ribbon to provide quick access to frequently used functionality.*

11. **XML and RibbonX:** *Ribbon customization is done using XML and RibbonX, a custom XML schema for extending the Ribbon. You can define the layout and behavior of your custom Ribbon elements using these technologies.*

Building Add-Ins

*12. **Creating Add-Ins:** Access lets you create custom add-ins that can be shared and used across multiple databases. Add-ins are a way to package your custom functionality, such as VBA code or custom Ribbon elements, for reuse.*

*13. **Deployment:** Once you've created an add-in, you can deploy it to other users or databases. This allows you to maintain consistency in your database applications by sharing your custom solutions.*

Integration with Other Office Applications

*14. **Integration:** Access seamlessly integrates with other Microsoft Office applications, such as Excel, Word, and Outlook. You can use VBA to automate interactions between these applications, sharing data and functionality.*

*15. **Access as a Data Source:** You can also use Access as a data source for other applications. This means you can pull data from your Access database into Excel for analysis, or use Access data in Word to generate customized reports.*

In the subsequent sections of this chapter, we will explore each of these topics in detail, providing you with the knowledge and skills to harness the full potential of Access automation and customization. Whether you need to streamline your workflow, enhance user experience, or extend Access functionality, these tools and techniques will be invaluable.

Section 6.5: Integrating Access with Other Office Applications

Microsoft Access is a versatile database management system that can seamlessly integrate with other Microsoft Office applications, enhancing its capabilities and allowing you to leverage the strengths of various Office tools. In this section, we will explore how Access can be integrated with Word, Excel, PowerPoint, and Outlook, opening up a world of possibilities for data sharing and automation.

Linking Data Across Applications

*1. **Importing and Exporting Data:** Access allows you to import data from Excel spreadsheets, text files, or other data sources. You can also export Access data to Excel, allowing for advanced data analysis, reporting, and visualization.*

*2. **Linking External Data:** Access enables you to create linked tables that connect to external data sources like SQL Server databases or SharePoint lists. This means you can work with data from other systems directly within your Access database.*

Embedding Excel Data in Word and PowerPoint

*3. **Embedding Excel Worksheets:** You can embed Excel worksheets into Word documents or PowerPoint presentations. This is useful when you want to include dynamic, data-driven tables or charts in your reports or slides.*

*4. **Updating Linked Data:** Embedded Excel data in Word or PowerPoint can be linked to an Access database or an external data source. When the underlying data changes, the linked content in your documents and presentations can be updated automatically.*

Using Access Data in Excel and Word

*5. **Exporting Access Queries and Reports:** Access allows you to export queries, tables, and reports to Excel or Word. This is helpful for generating reports with a polished layout in Word or conducting further data analysis in Excel.*

*6. **Mail Merge with Access Data:** Word offers mail merge functionality that can be connected to Access databases. This enables you to create personalized letters, emails, or labels by pulling data directly from Access.*

Dynamic Document Creation with Office

*7. **Automating Document Creation:** With the integration of Access and other Office applications, you can automate the generation of documents and reports. For example, you can create invoices, contracts, or reports using predefined templates and Access data.*

*8. **Data-Driven PowerPoint Presentations:** You can use Access data to generate dynamic PowerPoint presentations. This is valuable for creating sales presentations, performance reports, or any scenario where data needs to be presented visually.*

Collaborative Workflows Across Applications

*9. **Collaborative Editing:** Office 365 and SharePoint integration allows for real-time collaboration on Word, Excel, and PowerPoint documents. Access data can be part of this collaborative ecosystem, making it easier for teams to work together.*

10. *Task Automation:* By using VBA scripts, you can automate tasks that involve multiple Office applications. For instance, you can automate the process of exporting Access data to Excel, creating charts, and embedding them in a Word report.

Enhancing Efficiency and Productivity

Integrating Access with other Office applications offers numerous benefits, including enhanced efficiency, data consistency, and the ability to leverage the full capabilities of each tool. Whether you need to create data-driven reports in Word, perform complex analysis in Excel, create dynamic presentations in PowerPoint, or streamline communication in Outlook, Access integration can significantly improve your productivity.

In the following sections, we will explore practical examples and techniques for integrating Access with Word, Excel, PowerPoint, and Outlook, allowing you to harness the synergy of Microsoft Office for your database management tasks and business processes.

Chapter 7: OneNote for Organized Notes

Section 7.1: Getting Started with OneNote

Microsoft OneNote is a powerful note-taking and organization tool that allows users to capture and organize information in various formats, such as text, images, audio, and even handwritten notes. In this section, we will explore the basics of getting started with OneNote, from setting up your notebooks to creating and organizing your notes effectively.

Introduction to OneNote

*1. **Notebook Hierarchy:** OneNote is organized into a hierarchy of notebooks, sections, and pages. Notebooks are the top-level containers that hold your sections, and sections contain individual pages. This hierarchical structure provides a logical way to organize your notes.*

*2. **OneDrive Integration:** OneNote integrates with OneDrive, Microsoft's cloud storage service. This means your notebooks are automatically synced across your devices, ensuring that your notes are accessible from anywhere with an internet connection.*

Creating Your First Notebook

*3. **Creating a Notebook:** To create a new notebook, open OneNote and click on "File" > "New." You can choose to create the notebook on your local device or save it to OneDrive for cloud access.*

*4. **Naming and Saving:** Give your notebook a name and choose where you want to save it. If you save it to OneDrive, you'll have the advantage of syncing and accessing it across multiple devices.*

Sections and Pages

*5. **Sections:** Within a notebook, you can create sections to group related content. For example, you might have sections for "Meeting Notes," "Project Ideas," or "Personal Journal."*

*6. **Pages:** Pages are where you jot down your actual notes. You can create as many pages as needed within each section. OneNote offers a blank canvas for you to type, draw, add images, or insert other media.*

*7. **Organizing Sections and Pages:** OneNote provides simple drag-and-drop functionality to reorder sections and pages, making it easy to keep your content organized.*

Formatting Your Notes

*8. **Text Formatting:** Just like in other Office applications, you can format text in OneNote. Change fonts, colors, styles, and create bulleted or numbered lists to structure your notes.*

*9. **Tables and Tables of Contents:** OneNote supports tables, making it suitable for organizing data. You can also create a table of contents to navigate through your notes efficiently.*

Inserting Media

*10. **Images and Files:** You can insert images and files directly into your notes. This is handy for adding visual context or attaching documents related to your notes.*

*11. **Audio and Video:** OneNote allows you to record audio or video directly into your notes, making it an excellent choice for recording meetings or lectures.*

Handwriting and Drawing

*12. **Inking Tools:** If you have a touchscreen device or a digital pen, you can use OneNote's inking tools to write or draw on your notes naturally. Your handwritten notes are searchable within OneNote.*

Searching Your Notes

*13. **Powerful Search:** One of the standout features of OneNote is its powerful search capabilities. You can search for text, handwritten notes, and even text within images and scanned documents.*

Collaborative Notebooks

*14. **Sharing and Collaboration:** OneNote supports real-time collaboration. You can share notebooks with others, allowing multiple people to edit and contribute to the same set of notes simultaneously.*

*15. **Version History:** OneNote keeps a version history of your notebooks, so you can review changes, restore previous versions, and track the evolution of your notes over time.*

Mobile and Cross-Platform Access

*16. **Mobile Apps:** OneNote offers mobile apps for various platforms, including iOS and Android. This ensures that you can access and edit your notes on the go.*

*17. **Web Access:** If you're away from your devices, you can access your OneNote notebooks via a web browser by signing in to your OneDrive account.*

Getting started with OneNote is straightforward, and its flexibility makes it a versatile tool for personal and professional use. In the upcoming sections, we will explore advanced note-taking strategies, organization techniques, collaborative features, and ways to integrate OneNote with other Office applications for enhanced productivity.

Section 7.2: Effective Note-Taking Strategies

Taking effective notes is essential for maximizing the utility of Microsoft OneNote. While OneNote provides a flexible platform for note-taking, employing the right strategies can significantly enhance your productivity and organization. In this section, we will explore some effective note-taking strategies and tips to help you make the most out of OneNote.

1. Use a Consistent Structure:
- Create a standardized template for your notes. Consistency in formatting and layout makes it easier to review and search for information later.
- Consider using headings, subheadings, and bullet points to structure your notes logically.

2. Tagging and Labeling:

- OneNote offers a tagging feature that allows you to add labels like "Important," "To-Do," or "Question" to specific sections of your notes. Use tags to highlight key points and action items.

3. Linking and Cross-Referencing:

- Take advantage of OneNote's ability to link notes together. You can create hyperlinks between related notes or sections, making it easy to navigate your notebook.

4. Use Page Templates:

- Create custom page templates for recurring tasks or specific types of notes. Templates can save you time and ensure consistent formatting.

5. Handwriting and Drawing:

- If you have a touchscreen device or digital pen, consider using OneNote's inking tools for handwritten notes or drawings. OneNote's handwriting recognition can make your handwritten notes searchable.

6. Record Audio and Video:

- When attending lectures or meetings, record audio or video alongside your written notes. This feature helps capture nuances and ensures you don't miss important details.

7. Keep a Personal Dictionary:

- If you often use specific terminology or acronyms, create a personal dictionary within OneNote. This will help with quick definitions or explanations.

8. Clipboard Management:

- OneNote acts as a versatile clipboard. You can copy and paste text, images, or content from other sources directly into your notes. This is handy for research and information gathering.

9. Use Tables for Organization:

- Tables can be useful for organizing data within your notes. Whether it's creating a list of tasks, tracking project milestones, or comparing pros and cons, tables can help maintain clarity.

10. Search and Tagging for Reference:

- OneNote's robust search capabilities allow you to find specific notes quickly. Combine this with tags, and you can easily locate important information, even across multiple notebooks.

11. Backup and Sync:

- Regularly back up your OneNote notebooks and ensure they are synced to the cloud. This provides data security and allows you to access your notes from various devices.

12. Collaborative Note-Taking:
- If you are collaborating with others on the same notebook, use the collabor ation features effectively. Assign tasks, track changes, and communicate with in OneNote.

13. Review and Summarize:
- Periodically review your notes and create summaries or action plans. This h elps distill key insights and action items from your notes.

14. Handwriting Recognition:
- If you prefer to write notes by hand, take advantage of OneNote's handwriti ng recognition. It can convert your handwritten text into searchable, typed t ext.

15. Privacy and Security:
- Be mindful of sensitive information. OneNote offers password protection and encryption for sections or entire notebooks to safeguard confidential data.

Effective note-taking is a skill that can significantly impact your personal and professional life. With the flexibility and features offered by Microsoft OneNote, you can tailor your note-taking approach to suit your needs. Experiment with these strategies and adapt them to your workflow to make your note-taking in OneNote more efficient and organized.

Section 7.3: Organizing and Searching Notes

Effective organization and quick retrieval of information are vital aspects of using Microsoft OneNote. This section delves into strategies for organizing your notes and efficiently searching for specific content within your notebooks.

1. Notebook Structure:
- Begin by creating notebooks that reflect different areas of your life or work. For example, you might have separate notebooks for personal, professional, or project-specific notes.
- Within each notebook, use sections to categorize related content. Sections act as folders for grouping similar notes.

2. Page Hierarchy:
- Within sections, establish a hierarchy of pages. You can create subpages beneath main pages to further organize your notes.
- Use descriptive page titles that provide a clear overview of the page's content.

3. Table of Contents:
- Consider adding a table of contents to the beginning of each section. A table of contents page can serve as a quick reference to locate specific topics or pages within that section.

4. Tags and Labels:

- OneNote's tagging feature is a powerful tool for marking and categorizing notes. Use tags like "To-Do," "Important," or custom tags to identify and group notes by their significance or purpose.

5. Search Functionality:

- OneNote's search capabilities are robust. Use the search bar to find specific words or phrases across all your notebooks.
- You can also perform searches within a particular section, making it easier to narrow down results.

6. Keyword Consistency:

- Be consistent with the keywords you use within your notes. Using the same terminology for related topics helps streamline searches.
- If you have specific acronyms or jargon, ensure you use them consistently throughout your notes.

7. Audio and Video Search:

- If you've recorded audio or video in your notes, you can search for specific spoken words or phrases within these recordings. OneNote's audio and video search functionality is a valuable asset for content retrieval.

8. OCR for Images:

- OneNote can perform optical character recognition (OCR) on images with text. This means you can search for text within images or screenshots added to your notes.

9. Custom Sections and Labels:

- Create custom sections or labels that align with your specific needs. For instance, you might have sections for meeting notes, research, or project-related content.

10. Page Versions:

- OneNote retains versions of your pages. If you make significant changes to a page and later need to revert to a previous version, you can access the page history.

11. Use Links and Cross-References:

- Link related notes or pages together. This makes it easy to navigate between relevant content without relying solely on search.

12. Master Notebook Index:

- Create a master notebook or section that acts as an index to all your notebooks. This index can provide a bird's-eye view of your content and help you quickly locate the notebook you need.

13. Regular Maintenance:

- Periodically review and reorganize your notebooks and sections. Remove unnecessary or outdated content to maintain a clutter-free environment.

14. Tags Summary:
- OneNote can generate a summary page for specific tags, compiling all notes tagged with a particular keyword. This can serve as a handy reference for tasks or important points.

15. Backup and Sync:
- Ensure your OneNote notebooks are regularly backed up and synchronized across devices. This guarantees that you can access your organized notes from anywhere.

By implementing these strategies for organizing and searching your notes in OneNote, you can create a streamlined workflow that maximizes your productivity and ensures that your valuable information is always at your fingertips. Whether you're managing personal projects or collaborating in a team, effective organization and search functionality in OneNote are indispensable tools.

Section 7.4: Collaborative Notebooks

Collaboration is a key feature of Microsoft OneNote, allowing multiple users to work together on the same notebook simultaneously. In this section, we will explore how to set up and effectively collaborate within OneNote.

1. Shared Notebooks:
- To start collaborating, you need a shared notebook. You can create a new notebook and choose to share it with others by inviting them via email. Alternatively, you can work on a notebook stored on a shared platform like OneDrive or SharePoint.

2. Permissions:
- When sharing a notebook, you can assign different permissions to collaborators. These permissions include "View Only," "Edit," and "Edit and Invite Others." Assign permissions according to the level of access you want each collaborator to have.

3. Real-Time Editing:
- OneNote allows real-time editing, which means that you and your collaborators can make changes to the notebook simultaneously. Changes made by one user are instantly visible to others.

4. Version History:
- OneNote keeps a version history of your notebook. If a mistake is made or if you need to revert to a previous state, you can access the version history and restore an earlier version.

5. Page Locking:

- To avoid conflicts when multiple users are editing the same page, OneNote offers page locking. When a user starts editing a page, others can view it but not make changes until the page is unlocked.

6. Note Syncing:

- Collaborators' notes are automatically synced across devices. Whether they're using OneNote on a computer, tablet, or smartphone, everyone will have access to the latest updates.

7. Comments and Annotations:

- Collaborators can leave comments and annotations on specific parts of a page. This feature is useful for discussing changes or providing feedback without altering the original content.

8. Notifications:

- OneNote sends notifications to collaborators when changes are made. This keeps everyone informed about updates and ensures that no important edits go unnoticed.

9. Conflict Resolution:

- In cases where conflicting changes occur, OneNote provides conflict resolution tools. Collaborators can review and decide which version of the content to keep.

10. Shared Tags and Labels:

- Collaborators can use the same set of tags and labels for consistent note-taking. This enhances organization and helps in categorizing notes effectively.

11. Access Control:

- You can control who has access to the shared notebook at any time. If you need to revoke access for a specific user, you can do so from the sharing settings.

12. Offline Access:

- Collaborators can access shared notebooks even when they're offline. Once they reconnect to the internet, any changes they made offline will sync with the shared notebook.

13. Archiving and Backups:

- Regularly back up shared notebooks to prevent data loss. You can also archive completed projects or notebooks that are no longer actively edited.

14. Collaborative Workflows:

- OneNote's collaborative features are particularly useful for team projects, brainstorming sessions, and meeting notes. It streamlines communication and ensures that everyone is on the same page, literally.

15. Security and Privacy:
- Be mindful of security and privacy when sharing notebooks. Ensure that sensitive information is only shared with trusted collaborators, and use password protection when necessary.

Collaborative notebooks in OneNote open up a world of possibilities for teamwork and information sharing. Whether you're collaborating with colleagues, classmates, or friends, OneNote's real-time editing, version history, and communication features make it a valuable tool for collaborative note-taking and project management.

Section 7.5: Integrating OneNote with Other Office Tools

Integrating Microsoft OneNote with other Office applications can significantly enhance your productivity and streamline your work processes. In this section, we will explore various ways to integrate OneNote with other Office tools and maximize the benefits of this synergy.

1. OneNote and Outlook:
- OneNote and Outlook work seamlessly together. You can send emails or meeting details directly to OneNote, creating linked notes that reference specific messages or events. This is valuable for keeping track of important information and discussions.

2. OneNote and Word/Excel/PowerPoint:
- You can easily embed OneNote content into Word, Excel, or PowerPoint documents. This allows you to include notes, drawings, or screenshots from your OneNote notebooks directly into your reports, spreadsheets, or presentations.

3. OneNote and SharePoint/OneDrive:
- When you store your OneNote notebooks on SharePoint or OneDrive, you enable easy collaboration and access from anywhere. Multiple users can edit the same notebook simultaneously, and changes are automatically synced.

4. OneNote and Teams:
- Microsoft Teams integrates with OneNote, allowing you to create shared notebooks for your team's channels. This ensures that all team members have access to essential information, meeting notes, and project details.

5. OneNote and Forms:
- You can create forms and surveys using Microsoft Forms and then link the responses directly to OneNote. This is useful for gathering and organizing data and feedback.

6. OneNote and To-Do Lists:

- OneNote can be used to create detailed to-do lists and task management systems. You can integrate your to-do lists with Outlook tasks for better organization and tracking.

7. OneNote and Cortana:

- Cortana, Microsoft's virtual assistant, can be used to set reminders and create tasks in OneNote. It's a convenient way to keep track of deadlines and important dates.

8. OneNote and Planner:

- Microsoft Planner integrates with OneNote, allowing you to turn tasks into actionable items in your notebook. This is helpful for project management and tracking progress.

9. OneNote and Whiteboard:

- Microsoft Whiteboard can be linked to your OneNote notebooks, enabling you to brainstorm and draw together in real-time. The content created in Whiteboard can be easily inserted into your OneNote pages.

10. OneNote and Visio:

- If you use Microsoft Visio for creating diagrams and flowcharts, you can link your Visio diagrams to OneNote for detailed explanations and documentation.

11. OneNote and Power BI:

- OneNote can be used to keep track of your Power BI reports and dashboards. You can insert snapshots of your Power BI visualizations and add context or explanations.

12. OneNote and Excel Data:

- You can link Excel data directly to OneNote. When your Excel data changes, these updates will reflect in your OneNote notebook, ensuring your information is always up-to-date.

13. OneNote and Flow/Power Automate:

- With Microsoft Power Automate (formerly known as Flow), you can create workflows that trigger actions in OneNote based on specific events in other applications. This automation can save you time and effort.

14. OneNote and Third-Party Integrations:

- Many third-party apps and services offer integrations with OneNote. Explore the available integrations to find tools that enhance your productivity and meet your specific needs.

Integrating OneNote with other Office applications and services allows you to create a seamless and efficient workflow. Whether you're capturing information, collaborating with a team, or organizing your tasks, these integrations can help you work smarter and achieve more. Experiment with different integrations to discover the combination that best suits your work style and requirements.

Chapter 8: Collaborative Tools and Office 365

Section 8.1: Introduction to Office 365 and Its Capabilities

In today's digital workplace, collaboration is the key to productivity and success. Microsoft Office 365, commonly referred to as Office 365, is a cloud-based suite of applications and services designed to facilitate collaboration, communication, and productivity within organizations of all sizes. This section introduces you to the world of Office 365 and its capabilities, highlighting how it empowers teams to work more efficiently and effectively.

What is Office 365?

Office 365 is a subscription-based service offered by Microsoft that provides access to a wide range of productivity tools and services. It includes familiar applications like Word, Excel, PowerPoint, Outlook, and more, but it goes beyond individual productivity software. Office 365 is designed for teamwork and collaboration, making it an ideal choice for businesses and organizations that want to modernize their work environment.

Key Capabilities of Office 365:

1. **Cloud-Based Productivity:** One of the primary advantages of Office 365 is that it operates in the cloud. This means your documents, emails, and data are stored securely online, accessible from anywhere with an internet connection. It eliminates the need for on-premises servers and offers scalability to meet your organization's changing needs.

2. **Collaboration and Communication:** Office 365 provides a suite of communication tools, including Microsoft Teams, SharePoint, and Yammer. These tools enable real-time collaboration, instant messaging, file sharing, and video conferencing, fostering teamwork among remote and distributed teams.

3. **Always Up-to-Date:** With an Office 365 subscription, you always have access to the latest versions of Office applications and features. You no longer need to worry about manual software updates, ensuring you have the latest security patches and enhancements.

4. **Security and Compliance:** Microsoft takes security seriously, and Office 365 benefits from Microsoft's robust security infrastructure. It includes features like data loss prevention, threat protection, and compliance tools to keep your data safe and in compliance with industry regulations.

5. **Integration with Existing Tools:** Office 365 is designed to work seamlessly with your existing technology investments. Whether you use Windows, iOS, or Android, you can access and work with Office 365 applications on various devices.

6. **Flexibility and Scalability:** Office 365 offers various subscription plans tailored to different business needs. You can scale your subscription up or down as your organization grows or changes, ensuring cost-effectiveness.

To get started with Office 365, you need an active subscription and an internet connection. Users can access Office 365 applications through web browsers or by downloading and installing the desktop or mobile apps.

In subsequent sections of this chapter, we will delve deeper into specific Office 365 tools and how they can enhance collaboration, productivity, and communication within your organization. Whether you're a small business owner, an IT administrator, or an end-user, understanding Office 365's capabilities is essential for harnessing its full potential.

Section 8.2: Working in the Cloud: OneDrive and SharePoint

In this section, we will explore two fundamental components of Office 365 for cloud-based collaboration and file management: OneDrive and SharePoint. These services play a pivotal role in enabling teams to work together, share documents, and access their files from anywhere with an internet connection.

OneDrive for Business: Your Personal Cloud Storage

OneDrive for Business is an integral part of Office 365, offering each user a personal cloud storage space. It serves as a secure and convenient location to store and access your documents, spreadsheets, presentations, and other files. Here are some key features of OneDrive for Business:

1. **File Storage and Organization:** OneDrive allows you to upload, organize, and categorize your files and documents. You can create folders, move files, and even tag documents for easy retrieval.

2. **Sync Across Devices:** With OneDrive, your files are automatically synchronized across all your devices. Whether you're on your computer, tablet, or smartphone, you can access your files without manually transferring them.

3. **Real-Time Collaboration:** You can collaborate with colleagues by sharing files or folders with specific permissions. Multiple users can work on the same document simultaneously, making real-time edits and updates.

4. **Version History:** OneDrive keeps a record of changes made to documents, allowing you to view and restore previous versions if needed. This feature is invaluable for tracking document changes and maintaining a revision history.

5. **Security and Compliance:** OneDrive ensures the security of your files through robust encryption and compliance features. You can control who has access to your files and set expiration dates for shared links.

SharePoint Online is a comprehensive collaboration platform within Office 365 designed to facilitate teamwork, document sharing, and information management across organizations. Here's what you need to know about SharePoint Online:

1. **Team Sites:** SharePoint allows you to create team sites, which serve as dedicated spaces for groups or departments to collaborate. These sites can include document libraries, calendars, discussion boards, and more.

2. **Document Libraries:** SharePoint's document libraries are central repositories for storing and managing files. You can set up metadata, workflows, and access controls to ensure efficient document management.

3. **Workflow Automation:** SharePoint enables you to automate business processes and workflows, streamlining tasks such as document approvals, content publishing, and data collection.

4. **Intranet Portals:** SharePoint can be used to create intranet portals that serve as internal websites for sharing news, updates, and important information with employees.

5. **Customization:** SharePoint's flexibility allows you to customize your team sites and portals to meet specific organizational needs. You can add web parts, create custom lists, and use templates for consistency.

6. **Integration:** SharePoint seamlessly integrates with other Office 365 applications like Teams, OneDrive, and Outlook. This integration ensures a unified experience for users across various tools.

7. **Search and Discovery:** SharePoint's powerful search capabilities help users find the content they need quickly, whether it's documents, discussions, or people within the organization.

Both OneDrive and SharePoint complement each other, with OneDrive serving as a personal workspace and SharePoint providing a collaborative platform for teams and organizations. Together, they empower users to work efficiently in a cloud-based environment, making document sharing, collaboration, and information management more accessible than ever.

Section 8.3: Real-Time Collaboration and Communication

Real-time collaboration and communication are at the core of modern workplace productivity, and Office 365 offers a suite of tools to facilitate seamless interactions among team members. In this section, we'll explore the key components of Office 365 that enable real-time collaboration and communication.

Microsoft Teams: A Hub for Teamwork

Microsoft Teams is a unified communication and collaboration platform that brings together chat, video conferencing, file sharing, and app integration into a single workspace. Here are some essential aspects of Microsoft Teams:

1. **Chat and Messaging:** Teams provides chat functionality for one-on-one or group conversations. You can send text messages, share files, and even integrate external apps within chat conversations.

2. **Meetings and Video Conferencing:** Teams allows you to schedule and join online meetings and video conferences with colleagues, clients, or partners. Video calls, screen sharing, and recording options enhance collaboration.

3. **Channels:** Teams organizes conversations into channels, making it easy to separate discussions by topic, project, or department. Channels can also host tabs with apps and tools for specific needs.

4. **File Collaboration:** Teams integrates with SharePoint and OneDrive, making it effortless to share, edit, and collaborate on documents within the Teams interface. Multiple users can simultaneously edit documents in real-time.

5. **Integration with Office Apps:** You can integrate Office 365 apps directly into Teams, such as Word, Excel, PowerPoint, and Planner, to create, edit, and collaborate on documents without leaving the platform.

6. **Notifications and Activity Feed:** Teams keeps you informed with notifications about mentions, replies, and updates in your channels. The Activity feed provides an overview of recent activity in your teams and channels.

7. **Bots and Automation:** Teams supports the integration of bots and automation through the use of Microsoft Power Automate. You can create workflows to streamline repetitive tasks.

Yammer: Enterprise Social Networking

Yammer is an enterprise social networking tool that allows organizations to foster communication and collaboration across their workforce. Key features of Yammer include:

1. **Feed and Conversations:** Yammer provides a central feed where users can share updates, ask questions, and engage in discussions. It's an excellent platform for sharing knowledge and ideas.

2. **Groups and Communities:** Users can join or create groups and communities around specific topics, projects, or interests. This encourages collaboration among like-minded individuals.

3. **Announcements and Polls:** Yammer enables administrators to make important announcements to the entire organization. You can also create polls to gather feedback and opinions.

4. **Integration with SharePoint and Teams:** Yammer can be integrated with SharePoint and Teams, allowing users to access Yammer conversations within these platforms.

Outlook for Email and Calendar

Outlook is a familiar and robust email and calendar application within Office 365. It provides features for managing email communication and scheduling appointments and meetings. Some key elements of Outlook include:

1. **Email Management:** Outlook offers a powerful email client with features such as conversation view, focused inbox, and customizable rules to organize emails efficiently.

2. **Calendar and Scheduling:** The calendar in Outlook helps users schedule appointments, meetings, and events. It also supports features like shared calendars and resource booking.

3. **Task Management:** Outlook integrates with tasks and to-do lists, allowing users to manage their tasks and priorities within the same application.

4. **Integration with Teams:** Outlook integrates seamlessly with Microsoft Teams, making it easy to schedule and join Teams meetings directly from your calendar.

5. **Mobile Access:** Outlook is available on various platforms, including mobile devices, ensuring that you can stay connected and productive while on the go.

Real-time collaboration and communication tools in Office 365 are designed to enhance teamwork, streamline communication, and boost productivity. Whether you're working on a project, conducting virtual meetings, or engaging in discussions, these tools provide the flexibility and efficiency needed for modern work environments.

Section 8.4: Leveraging Teams for Group Work

Microsoft Teams is a powerful collaboration platform that plays a central role in Office 365 for group work and team communication. In this section, we'll delve into various aspects of leveraging Microsoft Teams for effective group work.

Creating and Managing Teams

Teams in Microsoft Teams are digital spaces where groups of people can collaborate and communicate. Here's how to create and manage teams:

1. **Create a Team:** To create a new team, click the "Teams" tab on the left sidebar and select "Join or create a team." You can choose to create a team from scratch or use a template. Teams can be private or public.

2. **Managing Members:** As the owner or a member of a team, you can add or remove members. Go to the team's settings, and under the "Members" tab, you can manage the team's membership.

3. **Channels:** Teams are organized into channels, which are like sections within a team for focused discussions. You can create channels for specific projects, topics, or departments.

4. **Tabs and Apps:** In each channel, you can add tabs for various apps and tools, including Planner, OneNote, SharePoint, and more. These tabs allow you to integrate essential tools directly into your team's workspace.

Chat and Collaboration

Microsoft Teams offers robust chat and collaboration features:

1. **Chat:** You can initiate one-on-one or group chats with team members. Chat messages support rich text formatting, file sharing, and emoji reactions.

2. **@Mentions:** Use "@mention" to get someone's attention in a chat or channel conversation. They will receive a notification.

3. **File Sharing:** Teams integrates with OneDrive and SharePoint, making it easy to share and collaborate on files. Multiple team members can edit a document simultaneously in real-time.

4. **Meetings:** You can schedule and join online meetings directly from Teams. Meetings support video conferencing, screen sharing, and recording.

Integration with Office Apps

One of the strengths of Microsoft Teams is its seamless integration with Office 365 apps:

1. **Word, Excel, PowerPoint:** You can create, edit, and collaborate on Office documents within Teams using the online versions of these apps.

2. **Planner:** Teams includes Planner, a tool for task management and project planning. You can create and assign tasks to team members right within your Teams channels.

3. **Power BI:** If your team works with data and analytics, you can integrate Power BI reports and dashboards into Teams for data visualization and analysis.

Notifications and Activity

To keep track of activity within your teams and channels:

1. **Activity Feed:** The "Activity" tab in Teams provides a centralized view of notifications, mentions, and recent activity across your teams and channels.

2. **Customize Notifications:** Teams allows you to customize notification settings for each team and channel, ensuring you stay informed without being overwhelmed.

Mobile Accessibility

Microsoft Teams is available as a mobile app, ensuring that you can stay connected and collaborate on the go. The mobile app provides a similar experience to the desktop version, including chat, meetings, and document access.

In summary, Microsoft Teams is a versatile platform that empowers teams to collaborate, communicate, and work together efficiently. It integrates seamlessly with other Office 365 apps and offers a range of features for managing teams, chat, collaboration, and notifications. Whether your team is working remotely or in the same office, Teams can significantly enhance productivity and teamwork.

Section 8.5: Mobile Productivity with Office Apps

Mobile productivity has become increasingly essential in today's fast-paced work environment. Microsoft offers a suite of Office apps for mobile devices, including smartphones and tablets, to ensure you can work efficiently while on the move.

Office Mobile Apps

Microsoft provides mobile versions of its popular Office applications, including Word, Excel, PowerPoint, Outlook, OneNote, and more. These apps are available for both iOS and Android devices and are designed to offer a seamless experience for creating, editing, and collaborating on documents.

1. **Microsoft Word Mobile:** With Word Mobile, you can view and edit Word documents on your mobile device. It retains most of the essential features of the desktop version, allowing you to format text, add images, and track changes.

2. **Microsoft Excel Mobile:** Excel Mobile enables you to work with spreadsheets on the go. You can create and edit Excel files, perform calculations, and use basic functions and formulas.

3. **Microsoft PowerPoint Mobile:** PowerPoint Mobile allows you to create and edit presentations, add slides, apply themes, and rehearse your presentations right from your mobile device.

4. **Microsoft Outlook Mobile:** Outlook Mobile is a powerful email and calendar app that helps you manage your emails, appointments, and contacts while on the move.

5. **OneNote Mobile:** Capture and organize your notes, ideas, and to-do lists with OneNote Mobile. It syncs seamlessly with the desktop and web versions of OneNote.

Key Features and Benefits

Here are some key features and benefits of using Office Mobile apps:

- **Cloud Integration:** Office Mobile apps are tightly integrated with OneDrive, SharePoint, and Office 365, ensuring your documents are accessible from anywhere and automatically synchronized across devices.

- **Cross-Platform Compatibility:** Whether you use an iPhone, iPad, Android phone, or tablet, Microsoft's Office Mobile apps are available and offer consistent functionality and formatting.

- **Offline Access:** You can work on your documents even without an internet connection. Changes will sync when you're back online.

- **Collaboration:** Office Mobile apps support real-time collaboration, allowing multiple users to work on the same document simultaneously. This is especially useful for team projects and remote work scenarios.

- **Touch-Friendly Interface:** The user interfaces of these apps are optimized for touch input, making it easy to navigate and interact with documents using your fingers or a stylus.

Tips for Mobile Productivity

To maximize your mobile productivity with Office apps:

1. **Use a Tablet or Larger Screen:** While Office Mobile apps are designed for smartphones, using a tablet with a larger screen can provide a more comfortable and efficient experience, especially for editing documents.

2. **Sync and Backup:** Ensure that your Office documents are regularly synced to the cloud and backed up to prevent data loss.

3. **Keyboard and Accessories:** If you frequently work on documents while on the move, consider using a Bluetooth keyboard and other accessories to enhance your productivity.

4. **Mobile Data Management:** Be mindful of your mobile data usage when working with cloud-based documents, especially when outside of Wi-Fi coverage.

5. **Security:** Implement security measures on your mobile device to protect sensitive information, such as setting up a PIN or using biometric authentication.

In conclusion, Microsoft's Office Mobile apps empower users to remain productive while away from their desks. With a wide range of features and seamless integration with Office 365 and cloud services, you can work efficiently, collaborate with others, and access your documents whenever and wherever you need them. Whether you're a business professional, student, or freelancer, these mobile apps are valuable tools for maintaining productivity on the go.

Chapter 9: Advanced Word Techniques

Section 9.1: Mastering Mail Merge and Form Letters

In Microsoft Word, the Mail Merge feature is a powerful tool that allows you to create customized documents, such as form letters, envelopes, labels, and more, by merging a document template with a data source. This capability is especially useful for tasks like sending personalized letters to a list of recipients, generating address labels for a mailing list, or creating individualized certificates.

Understanding Mail Merge

Before diving into the specifics of Mail Merge, let's understand its key components:

- **Main Document:** This is your document template, which contains the text and formatting that will remain the same in every copy of the merged document. It includes placeholders, called merge fields, that will be replaced with data from your data source.

- **Data Source:** The data source can be an Excel spreadsheet, a Microsoft Access database, an Outlook contact list, or even a simple text file. It contains the information you want to merge into your main document. Each column in the data source typically corresponds to a merge field in the main document.

- **Merge Fields:** These are placeholders in your main document where data from the data source will be inserted. For example, you might have a merge field like <> that will be replaced with the actual first name of each recipient.

Creating a Mail Merge

To perform a mail merge in Word:

1. **Open your main document:** Start with a blank document or an existing one, and make sure it includes the necessary text and formatting.

2. **Select the type of document:** Choose what type of document you want to create, such as letters, envelopes, labels, or directories. Word will guide you through the process based on your selection.

3. **Connect to your data source:** Link your main document to your data source by selecting "Select Recipients" or "Use an Existing List." Follow the prompts to locate and connect to your data source.

4. **Insert merge fields:** Place your cursor where you want to insert a merge field, then select "Insert Merge Field" and choose the appropriate field from your data source.

5. **Preview your merge:** Use the "Preview Results" button to see how the merged document will look for different records in your data source.

6. **Complete the merge:** Click "Finish & Merge" and choose an option such as printing the documents directly, creating a new document with the merged results, or sending them via email.

While the basic steps cover most mail merge needs, there are advanced techniques you can explore:

- **Conditional Content:** You can use IF statements in your merge fields to include or exclude content based on specific conditions. For example, you can include a greeting only if the recipient's gender is known.

- **Sorting and Filtering:** Before merging, you can sort and filter your data source to include specific records. This is handy for targeted mailings.

- **Formatting and Styles:** Apply different formatting and styles to merge fields to make them stand out or match your document's design.

- **Mail Merge with Labels:** When creating labels, Word provides options to select label types and adjust layout settings.

- **Using Excel as a Data Source:** Excel is a common choice for data sources. You can connect Word to an Excel workbook and use Excel's functionality for data management.

- **Merged Emails:** Besides printed documents, you can use Mail Merge to send personalized email messages to a list of recipients. This is particularly useful for email marketing campaigns.

- **Data Source Editing:** You can edit your data source within Word, allowing you to make changes or additions without leaving the application.

Tips and Best Practices

Here are some tips for successful Mail Merge:

- **Test Before Finalizing:** Always test your merge with a small set of data to ensure everything appears as expected before executing it for the entire list.

- **Data Cleanup:** Ensure your data source is clean and consistent to prevent formatting issues during the merge.

- **Backup Data:** Make a backup of your data source before performing a merge, especially if you plan to make extensive changes to the merged documents.

- **Review Merged Output:** After merging, carefully review the final documents to catch any errors or formatting issues.

Mail Merge is a versatile feature in Microsoft Word that can save you significant time and effort when dealing with bulk documents or personalized communications. Whether you're sending out invitations, generating reports, or managing a mailing list, mastering Mail Merge can streamline the process and enhance your document production efficiency.

Section 9.2: Long Document Management

When working on long and complex documents in Microsoft Word, such as reports, research papers, manuals, or novels, efficient document management becomes essential. Managing content, formatting, and structure for lengthy documents can be challenging, but Word offers several tools and techniques to make the process smoother.

Structuring Your Document

1. **Use Styles:** Styles are pre-defined sets of formatting settings that you can apply to headings, paragraphs, and other elements in your document. Utilizing styles consistently for headings and body text not only ensures a professional appearance but also makes it easier to generate a table of contents and maintain document structure.

2. **Headings and Subheadings:** Break your document into sections with clear headings and subheadings. Word's built-in heading styles (e.g., Heading 1, Heading 2) are handy for this purpose. You can create a table of contents based on these headings, allowing readers to navigate your document easily.

3. **Navigation Pane:** The Navigation Pane in Word provides an outline view of your document's structure based on headings. It allows you to quickly jump to different sections and reorganize content as needed.

4. **Document Map:** If you're working with very long documents, consider using the Document Map feature. It provides a dynamic summary of your document's structure in a separate pane, making it easy to navigate and rearrange sections.

Document Organization

1. **Page Breaks:** Use page breaks to start new sections or chapters on fresh pages. You can insert page breaks manually or let Word handle them automatically based on your document structure.

2. **Table of Contents (TOC):** If your document contains multiple sections and headings, create a table of contents using Word's built-in TOC feature. It automatically generates a clickable list of all your headings, providing easy navigation for readers.

3. **Footnotes and Endnotes:** When dealing with references or additional information, consider using footnotes or endnotes rather than cluttering the main text. Word allows you to manage footnotes and endnotes efficiently.

4. **Sections:** In Word, you can divide your document into sections, each with its own formatting settings (e.g., margins, headers, footers). This is useful for creating different layouts within the same document, such as landscape-oriented pages in a portrait-oriented document.

Collaboration and Review

1. **Track Changes:** When collaborating with others on a lengthy document, enable Track Changes. This feature records all edits, comments, and suggestions made by reviewers. You can accept or reject changes and review comments within the document.

2. **Comments:** Use comments to leave notes for yourself or others within the document. Comments are a great way to jot down thoughts, reminders, or explanations without altering the main text.

3. **Reviewing Pane:** The Reviewing Pane provides a side-by-side view of the document with tracked changes and comments, making it easier to navigate through edits and feedback.

Performance Optimization

1. **Page Numbers:** Ensure your document's page numbering is consistent and properly aligned. Word offers options to control page numbering formats and starting points.

2. **Table of Figures and Tables:** If your document contains numerous figures and tables, create separate tables of figures and tables. This helps readers locate specific visuals more efficiently.

3. **Compact View:** When reviewing or editing a lengthy document, use Word's Compact View option to see more content on the screen, reducing the need for constant scrolling.

Document Protection

1. **Document Security:** If your document contains sensitive information, consider protecting it with a password or restricting editing permissions. Word provides various security features to safeguard your content.

2. **Backup and Recovery:** Regularly save backups of your document to prevent data loss. Word's AutoSave and AutoRecover features can help recover unsaved changes in case of unexpected interruptions.

Efficiently managing long documents in Microsoft Word involves a combination of proper structuring, organization, collaboration, and optimization. By using the features and techniques mentioned above, you can create, edit, and maintain lengthy documents with ease while ensuring a professional and polished final product.

Section 9.3: Custom Graphics and SmartArt

In Microsoft Word, incorporating custom graphics and utilizing SmartArt can enhance the visual appeal and clarity of your documents. Whether you're creating a report, presentation, or brochure, visuals can help convey information effectively. This section covers the insertion and customization of graphics, as well as the use of SmartArt for illustrating ideas and concepts.

Inserting Images and Graphics

1. **Insert Picture:** To insert an image or graphic, go to the "Insert" tab and select "Picture." Browse your computer or online sources for the image you want to include. Word supports various image formats, including JPEG, PNG, GIF, and more.

2. **Resize and Crop:** After inserting an image, you can resize it by clicking and dragging its corners. To crop an image, select it and choose the "Crop" option from the "Format" tab. This allows you to focus on specific parts of the image.

3. **Positioning and Wrapping:** Use the "Position" options to control how text flows around your image. You can choose to have text wrap around the image, move it inline with text, or position it freely.

4. **Alignment and Spacing:** To align images precisely or adjust their spacing relative to text, access the "Alignment" and "Spacing" options in the "Format" tab. This is particularly useful when working with multiple images or objects.

Using SmartArt Graphics

1. **Insert SmartArt:** SmartArt is a feature that allows you to create visually appealing diagrams and charts. To insert SmartArt, go to the "Insert" tab, select "SmartArt," and choose a graphic type that suits your content, such as a hierarchy, process, or cycle diagram.

2. **Adding and Editing Shapes:** Once you've inserted SmartArt, you can add shapes and text to represent your ideas. Click on the SmartArt graphic, and the "SmartArt Design" and "Format" tabs will appear. Use these tabs to add shapes, change their order, and edit text within each shape.

3. **Style and Layout:** SmartArt comes with various styles and layouts. Experiment with different styles to find the one that matches your document's visual theme. You can also change the layout of your SmartArt graphic to emphasize different aspects of your content.

4. **Color and Effects:** Customize the colors and effects of your SmartArt graphic to make it visually appealing and in line with your document's design. The "Change Colors" and "Change Effects" options can be found in the "SmartArt Design" tab.

1. **Inserting Charts:** Word also allows you to insert charts and graphs to present data visually. Go to the "Insert" tab, select "Chart," and choose the type of chart that best represents your data, such as bar, pie, or line charts.

2. **Data Source and Editing:** After inserting a chart, you can link it to an Excel spreadsheet or manually input data. Clicking on the chart will display "Chart Tools" tabs for "Design," "Format," and "Chart." Use these tabs to edit data, customize the chart style, and add labels.

3. **Updating Charts:** If your data changes, you can easily update the chart by editing the linked data source in Excel or by manually modifying the data in Word. The chart will automatically reflect the changes.

4. **Chart Elements:** Customize your chart by adding elements like data labels, titles, and legends. These elements help explain the chart's content to the reader.

Accessibility Considerations

When using custom graphics, images, and SmartArt in your documents, it's crucial to consider accessibility. Ensure that you provide alternative text descriptions for images to make your content accessible to individuals with disabilities. In Word, you can add alt text by right-clicking on an image and selecting "Edit Alt Text."

In summary, incorporating custom graphics and utilizing SmartArt in Microsoft Word can significantly enhance the visual impact and clarity of your documents. Whether you're adding images, creating diagrams, or visualizing data, Word offers a range of tools and options to help you create visually appealing and informative content.

Section 9.4: Word's Advanced Reference Features

Microsoft Word provides advanced reference features that can help you create professional and well-structured documents. These features allow you to manage citations, create bibliographies, cross-reference content, and generate tables of contents. In this section, we'll explore these advanced reference tools.

Citations and Bibliographies

1. **Inserting Citations:** Word allows you to insert citations and references from various sources, including books, articles, and websites. To do this, go to the "References" tab and click on "Insert Citation." You can add, edit, or manage your sources using the built-in citation manager.

2. **Choosing Citation Styles:** Word supports different citation styles, such as APA, MLA, Chicago, and more. You can select your preferred citation style in the "Citation

Style" dropdown menu. Word will automatically format citations and bibliographies according to your chosen style.

3. **Creating a Bibliography:** To generate a bibliography or list of references, place your cursor where you want the bibliography to appear and click on "Bibliography" in the "References" tab. Word will create a formatted list of all the sources you've cited in your document.

Cross-Referencing Content

1. **Cross-Referencing Headings:** Word allows you to cross-reference headings, figures, tables, equations, and more within your document. This is especially useful for creating dynamic documents like reports and manuals. To cross-reference, go to the "References" tab and click on "Cross-reference."

2. **Choosing Reference Types:** When you insert a cross-reference, you can choose from various reference types, including headings, figures, tables, equations, bookmarks, and more. Word will automatically update these references if the content they point to changes.

3. **Updating Cross-References:** To update all cross-references in your document, select the entire document (Ctrl + A) and press F9. This ensures that all references are up to date, reflecting any changes in your content.

Tables of Contents (TOC)

1. **Automatic TOC:** Word allows you to generate an automatic table of contents based on the headings in your document. To insert a TOC, place your cursor where you want it to appear (usually at the beginning of your document) and go to the "References" tab. Click on "Table of Contents" and choose a format from the provided options.

2. **Customizing TOC Styles:** You can customize the appearance and formatting of your TOC by modifying the built-in styles. To do this, right-click on the TOC and choose "Edit Field." Here, you can adjust settings like font size, indentation, and more.

3. **Updating the TOC:** If you add or reorganize headings in your document, you can update the TOC by right-clicking on it and selecting "Update Field." Word will automatically adjust the TOC to match the current document structure.

Footnotes and Endnotes

1. **Inserting Footnotes/Endnotes:** Word allows you to add footnotes or endnotes to provide additional information, explanations, or references within your document. To insert footnotes, go to the "References" tab and click on "Insert Footnote." You can choose between footnotes or endnotes in the dropdown menu.

2. **Customizing Note Formats:** You can customize the format of footnotes and endnotes, including the numbering style, position (bottom of the page or end of the document), and separator options. These settings can be adjusted in the "Footnote and Endnote" dialog box.

3. **Navigating Footnotes/Endnotes:** Word provides features for easy navigation between footnotes and endnotes in your document. You can use the navigation options in the "References" tab to jump to and edit specific notes.

In conclusion, Microsoft Word's advanced reference features empower you to create well-organized, professional documents. Whether you need to manage citations and bibliographies, cross-reference content, generate tables of contents, or work with footnotes and endnotes, Word offers a range of tools and customization options to streamline your document creation process.

Section 9.5: Automating Tasks with Macros

Microsoft Word provides a powerful feature called Macros that allows you to automate repetitive tasks and streamline your document creation process. Macros are essentially a series of recorded actions that can be replayed with a single click or keyboard shortcut. In this section, we'll explore how to create and use Macros effectively in Word.

Recording a Macro

1. **Enable the Developer Tab:** Before you can create Macros, you need to enable the Developer tab. To do this, go to "File" > "Options" > "Customize Ribbon." Check the "Developer" option, and click "OK."

2. **Record a Macro:** Once the Developer tab is visible, click on it and select "Record Macro." A dialog box will appear where you can name your Macro, assign a shortcut key (if desired), and choose where to store it (in the document or in the global template).

3. **Perform Actions:** With the Macro recording started, perform the actions you want to automate. This can include formatting, inserting content, or any other task you want to repeat later.

4. **Stop Recording:** After you've completed the actions, go back to the Developer tab and click on "Stop Recording." Your Macro is now saved and can be replayed at any time.

Running a Macro

1. **Open the Macros Dialog:** To run a Macro, go to the Developer tab and click on "Macros." A dialog box will appear, listing all available Macros in your document or template.

2. **Select and Run:** Choose the Macro you want to run from the list and click "Run." The recorded actions will be executed, automating the task for you.

3. **Assign a Button or Keyboard Shortcut:** You can make running Macros even more convenient by assigning them to a button or creating a keyboard shortcut. To assign

a Macro to a button, go to "File" > "Options" > "Customize Ribbon" and add a new group to a ribbon tab. Then, drag and drop the Macro onto that group.

Editing and Managing Macros

1. **View and Edit Macros:** You can view and edit Macros by going to the Developer tab, clicking on "Macros," and selecting "Edit." This allows you to modify the recorded actions or assign a new name and shortcut.

2. **Delete Macros:** If you no longer need a Macro, you can delete it from the Macros dialog box. Select the Macro and click "Delete."

3. **Macro Security:** It's important to note that Macros can pose a security risk if they come from untrusted sources. Word has built-in security settings that allow you to control the execution of Macros. Be cautious when enabling Macros in documents from unknown or untrusted sources.

Advanced Macros with VBA

For more advanced automation, Word offers Visual Basic for Applications (VBA), a powerful scripting language. With VBA, you can create complex Macros that involve logic, variables, loops, and more. To access the VBA editor, go to the Developer tab, click on "Visual Basic," and start writing or editing VBA code.

In conclusion, Macros in Microsoft Word are a valuable tool for automating repetitive tasks and improving your document workflow. By recording and running Macros, you can save time and reduce the risk of errors in your documents. For more advanced automation and customization, consider exploring Visual Basic for Applications (VBA), which opens up a world of possibilities for creating custom Macros tailored to your specific needs.

Chapter 10: Excel Data Management and Analysis

Section 10.1: Advanced Charting and Graphing

In Microsoft Excel, creating meaningful and visually appealing charts and graphs is essential for presenting and analyzing data effectively. While Excel offers a wide range of chart types and customization options, this section will delve into advanced charting techniques to help you take your data visualization skills to the next level.

Understanding Chart Elements

Before we explore advanced charting techniques, let's briefly review the key elements of an Excel chart:

- **Chart Title:** Provides context for the chart.
- **Axis Labels:** Describe the data points on the horizontal and vertical axes.
- **Data Series:** Represents the actual data you want to visualize.
- **Legend:** Explains the meaning of different data series or elements in the chart.
- **Gridlines:** Aid in reading values from the chart.
- **Data Labels:** Display specific data points' values.

Creating Advanced Charts

1. **Custom Chart Types:** Excel offers a variety of chart types beyond the basic bar, line, and pie charts. You can explore options like scatter plots, bubble charts, radar charts, and more. To create these, select your data and go to the "Insert" tab, then choose the chart type from the dropdown menu.

2. **Combining Chart Types:** Sometimes, a single chart type may not effectively represent your data. In Excel, you can create combination charts that combine two or more chart types in a single chart. For example, you could combine a bar chart with a line chart to visualize both quantities and trends.

3. **Secondary Axes:** When you have data with different units or scales, you can use a secondary axis to display two data series with distinct value ranges on the same chart. To add a secondary axis, select the data series you want to move, right-click, and choose "Format Data Series." In the "Series Options" section, select "Secondary Axis."

Enhancing Chart Visuals

1. **Themes and Styles:** Excel provides built-in chart themes and styles that allow you to quickly change the appearance of your chart. You can access these options through the "Chart Design" tab.

2. **Chart Elements and Formatting:** Customize your chart further by adding or removing elements like data labels, data tables, trendlines, or error bars. You can

also format elements such as fonts, colors, and borders by selecting the desired element and using the "Format" tab.

3. **3D Effects and Rotation:** To create a more visually striking chart, consider applying 3D effects or rotating your chart. Be cautious with 3D effects, as they can sometimes distort data representation. You can access these options through the "Format Chart Area" dialog.

Data Labels and Annotations

1. **Data Labels:** Data labels can provide clarity by displaying specific data points' values directly on the chart. You can add data labels by selecting the data series and using the "Data Labels" option in the "Chart Elements" dropdown.

2. **Annotations:** To draw attention to specific data points or trends, you can use annotations such as text boxes, shapes, or arrows. These can be added from the "Insert" tab and placed strategically on the chart.

Interactive Charts

1. **Excel Tables:** Convert your data into an Excel Table by selecting it and pressing "Ctrl+T." Tables offer dynamic data ranges that automatically update in the chart when you add or remove data.

2. **Slicers and Timelines:** Slicers and timelines are interactive elements that allow you to filter data in your chart. They are particularly useful for dashboards and reports. You can insert slicers and timelines from the "Insert" tab.

Advanced Charting with VBA

For highly customized and interactive charts, consider using Visual Basic for Applications (VBA). VBA allows you to create complex charting solutions and automate chart-related tasks. You can access the VBA editor by pressing "Alt+F11" and then create or edit VBA code to manipulate charts.

In conclusion, mastering advanced charting and graphing techniques in Excel enables you to convey your data's insights more effectively and create compelling visual representations. Whether you're presenting business trends, scientific data, or financial reports, Excel's advanced charting capabilities empower you to make a lasting impact with your audience.

Section 10.2: PivotTables and PivotCharts

PivotTables and PivotCharts are powerful tools in Microsoft Excel for data analysis and visualization. They allow you to summarize, analyze, and present data from different perspectives, making it easier to derive insights from large datasets. In this section, we'll explore how to create and work with PivotTables and PivotCharts effectively.

To create a PivotTable, follow these steps:

1. **Select Data:** Choose the dataset you want to analyze. This data should be organized with clear column headers.

2. **Insert PivotTable:** Go to the "Insert" tab and click "PivotTable." Excel will automatically select the data range based on your selection. Ensure the "Create PivotTable" dialog box appears.

3. **Choose Fields:** In the "Create PivotTable" dialog, you'll see a list of fields from your dataset. Drag and drop fields into the "Rows" and "Values" areas to define your PivotTable structure. For example, you can put a "Product" field in "Rows" and "Sales" in "Values" to see sales data by product.

4. **Customize Layout:** You can further customize the layout of your PivotTable by dragging fields between different areas or applying filters. Experiment with different field arrangements to see the data from various angles.

5. **Summarize Data:** Excel will automatically summarize your data using functions like SUM, COUNT, or AVERAGE. You can change the summary function by clicking on the drop-down arrow next to a value field in the "Values" area.

Working with PivotTable Features

PivotTables offer several features to enhance your data analysis:

- **Grouping:** You can group data by date, number ranges, or custom criteria. Right-click on a date field in the PivotTable, choose "Group," and set the grouping parameters.

- **Calculated Fields:** Create custom calculations based on your dataset by adding calculated fields. This can be useful for deriving new insights from your data.

- **Slicers:** Slicers are interactive filters that allow you to filter PivotTable data with ease. You can insert slicers from the "Insert" tab, and they work well for creating dynamic reports.

Creating a PivotChart

PivotCharts complement PivotTables by providing visual representations of your data. Here's how to create a PivotChart:

1. **Select PivotTable Data:** Start with an existing PivotTable or create a new one.

2. **Insert PivotChart:** With the PivotTable selected, go to the "Insert" tab and click "PivotChart." Excel will open the "Insert Chart" dialog.

3. **Choose Chart Type:** In the "Insert Chart" dialog, select the chart type you want to use. Common options include bar charts, line charts, and pie charts.

4. **Customize Chart:** Customize your PivotChart as needed. You can drag and drop fields into the chart's axis areas to define what data the chart represents. You can also change the chart style and format.

5. **Interact with PivotChart:** Just like PivotTables, PivotCharts can be interactive. Click on elements in the chart to filter data in real-time. This feature is particularly useful for exploring data from different angles.

Best Practices for PivotTables and PivotCharts

- **Keep Data Clean:** Ensure your dataset is well-structured with meaningful column headers. Avoid blank rows or columns.

- **Refresh Data:** If your dataset changes, remember to refresh your PivotTable or PivotChart to reflect the latest information.

- **Use PivotTable Styles:** Excel offers predefined styles for PivotTables that can make your reports look more professional. Experiment with different styles to find the one that suits your needs.

- **Practice Filtering:** PivotTables and PivotCharts become even more powerful when you learn how to filter and slice data effectively. Practice using filters and slicers to extract specific insights from your data.

In conclusion, PivotTables and PivotCharts are indispensable tools for data analysis and visualization in Excel. They empower you to transform raw data into actionable insights and communicate your findings effectively. By mastering these features and exploring their various options, you can become a proficient data analyst and presenter in Excel.

Section 10.3: Data Validation and Conditional Formatting

Data validation and conditional formatting are essential tools in Microsoft Excel that help you maintain data integrity, improve data accuracy, and enhance the visual presentation of your spreadsheets. In this section, we will explore how to use data validation to control input and how to apply conditional formatting to highlight data based on specific criteria.

Data Validation

Data validation allows you to set rules and restrictions on what can be entered into a cell. It ensures that data entered meets specific criteria or falls within predefined limits. Here's how to apply data validation:

1. **Select a Cell or Range:** Start by selecting the cell or range where you want to apply data validation.

2. **Access Data Validation:** Go to the "Data" tab and click on "Data Validation" in the "Data Tools" group. This will open the "Data Validation" dialog box.

3. **Set Validation Criteria:** In the dialog box, you can define various criteria such as whole numbers, decimals, dates, or custom formulas. For example, you can restrict a cell to accept only numbers between 1 and 100.

4. **Input Message (Optional):** You can provide an optional input message to guide users on what to enter. This message will appear as a tooltip when the cell is selected.

5. **Error Alert (Optional):** You can set up an error message to display if users enter data that doesn't meet the validation criteria. This can be useful for providing feedback and preventing invalid data entry.

6. **Save and Apply:** After configuring the data validation settings, click "OK" to apply the validation to the selected cells or range.

Data validation helps maintain data consistency and reduces the risk of errors in your Excel sheets. It's particularly useful when you have multiple users entering data into the same workbook.

Conditional Formatting

Conditional formatting allows you to change the appearance of cells based on specific conditions or rules. This helps highlight important information and make data easier to interpret. Here's how to use conditional formatting:

1. **Select Cells:** Start by selecting the cells you want to apply conditional formatting to. You can choose a single cell, a range, or an entire column.

2. **Access Conditional Formatting:** Go to the "Home" tab, and in the "Styles" group, click on "Conditional Formatting." This will open a menu with various formatting options.

3. **Choose a Rule:** From the menu, select the type of rule you want to apply. For example, you can choose "Highlight Cells Rules" to highlight values greater than a specific number.

4. **Set Formatting Options:** After selecting a rule, configure the formatting options. This may include specifying the condition (e.g., greater than, equal to) and choosing the formatting style (e.g., fill color, font color).

5. **Preview:** You can preview how the formatting will look in your selected cells before applying it.

6. **Apply Rule:** Click "OK" to apply the conditional formatting rule to the selected cells.

Conditional formatting can be used for various purposes, such as identifying outliers, visualizing trends, or emphasizing key data points. It helps make your data more visually appealing and easier to analyze.

- Use data validation to prevent invalid data entry and ensure data consistency.

- Provide clear input messages and error alerts when setting up data validation rules to guide users effectively.

- Experiment with different conditional formatting rules and styles to find the most effective way to visualize your data.

- Remember that data validation and conditional formatting are not mutually exclusive; you can use them together to create comprehensive data validation solutions.

- Regularly review and update data validation rules and conditional formatting as your data and reporting needs change.

In summary, data validation and conditional formatting are valuable tools in Excel for maintaining data quality and enhancing data visualization. Whether you need to control data input or highlight specific information, mastering these features will improve your Excel proficiency and the overall quality of your spreadsheets.

Section 10.4: Excel as a Tool for Financial Analysis

Microsoft Excel is a powerful tool for performing financial analysis, modeling, and calculations. Whether you're a financial analyst, accountant, or business professional, Excel offers a wide range of functions and features to help you make informed financial decisions. In this section, we will explore how to leverage Excel for various financial tasks.

Financial Functions

Excel provides a rich set of financial functions that allow you to perform complex calculations related to investments, loans, interest rates, and more. Some commonly used financial functions include:

- **NPV (Net Present Value):** Calculates the net present value of an investment based on a series of future cash flows and a discount rate.

- **IRR (Internal Rate of Return):** Determines the internal rate of return for an investment, indicating its profitability.

- **PMT (Payment):** Calculates the periodic payment for a loan or investment based on a fixed interest rate and term.

- **FV (Future Value):** Computes the future value of an investment or savings based on periodic contributions and interest rates.

- **PV (Present Value):** Determines the present value of future cash flows, helping in investment valuation.

- **RATE:** Calculates the interest rate for a loan or investment based on periodic payments and the present value.

These functions are essential for financial modeling, valuation, and decision-making. You can find them in Excel's "Formulas" tab under the "Financial" category.

Financial Modeling

Excel is widely used for creating financial models that simulate real-world financial scenarios. Financial models can help businesses forecast future performance, evaluate investment opportunities, and make strategic decisions. Some common types of financial models include:

- **Budget Models:** Used for creating annual budgets and tracking actual expenses against planned budgets.

- **Valuation Models:** Estimate the value of a company, asset, or investment based on financial projections and assumptions.

- **Cash Flow Models:** Analyze and forecast cash flows for a business, project, or investment.

- **Scenario Analysis:** Model different scenarios to assess the impact of various factors on financial outcomes.

Excel's ability to perform complex calculations, create charts and graphs, and support scenario analysis makes it an ideal tool for financial modeling. It offers flexibility and customization options to tailor models to specific needs.

Data Analysis Tools

Excel provides several data analysis tools that are valuable for financial professionals. These tools include:

- **Data Tables:** Analyze data by creating one-variable or two-variable data tables to perform sensitivity analysis.

- **Solver:** Optimize financial models by finding the best solution to achieve specific goals, such as maximizing profit or minimizing costs.

- **Goal Seek:** Determine the input value required to achieve a desired outcome in a financial model.

- **Scenario Manager:** Create and manage different scenarios within a financial model to assess various situations.

- **Regression Analysis:** Analyze relationships between variables and make predictions based on historical data.

These tools are particularly useful when dealing with large datasets and complex financial scenarios. They help streamline data analysis and decision-making processes.

Charting and Visualization

Effective data visualization is crucial in financial analysis to communicate insights and trends. Excel offers a variety of chart types, including line charts, bar charts, pie charts, and scatter plots, to help you visualize financial data. You can also create interactive dashboards using Excel's features, such as slicers and pivot tables, to explore and analyze financial information.

Data Import and Integration

Excel allows you to import data from external sources, such as databases, text files, and online sources, making it easier to work with diverse financial data. Additionally, you can integrate Excel with other Microsoft Office applications and tools like Power Query and Power Pivot for more advanced data analysis and reporting.

Auditing and Error Checking

Financial accuracy is crucial, and Excel provides auditing tools like the "Trace Dependents" and "Trace Precedents" functions to help you identify and fix errors in your financial models. You can also use the "Error Checking" feature to review formulas and resolve potential issues.

In conclusion, Excel is a versatile and indispensable tool for financial professionals. Its financial functions, modeling capabilities, data analysis tools, visualization features, and integration options make it a preferred choice for financial analysis, reporting, and decision-making in various industries. By mastering Excel's financial capabilities, you can enhance your financial expertise and improve your ability to make informed financial decisions.

Section 10.5: Solving Complex Problems with What-If Analysis

Excel's "What-If" analysis tools are powerful features that enable you to explore various scenarios and solve complex problems. They are particularly valuable for decision-making and planning in different domains, including finance, business, and engineering. In this section, we will delve into the "What-If" analysis tools available in Excel.

Goal Seek

Goal Seek is a built-in Excel tool that allows you to determine the input value needed to achieve a desired result. It is commonly used when you know the outcome you want but need to find the corresponding input. Here's how it works:

1. Start with a cell that contains a formula whose result you want to change (e.g., a financial model's NPV or IRR).

2. Go to the "Data" tab and click on "What-If Analysis."

3. Select "Goal Seek" from the dropdown menu.

4. In the Goal Seek dialog box, specify the cell containing the formula you want to change (the "Set Cell").

5. Set the desired value you want the formula to produce (the "To Value").

6. Specify the cell that you want to change to achieve the desired result (the "By Changing Cell").

7. Click "OK," and Excel will calculate the required input value to reach your goal.

Goal Seek is incredibly useful for solving problems where you need to back-calculate an input based on a desired output. For instance, you can use it to determine the required sales volume to achieve a specific profit margin.

Scenario Manager

Scenario Manager is a tool for creating and managing different scenarios within your Excel workbook. It's beneficial when you want to compare how changes in specific variables affect your results. Here's how to use it:

1. Define a base scenario with your initial data and assumptions.

2. Go to the "Data" tab and click on "What-If Analysis."

3. Select "Scenario Manager" from the dropdown menu.

4. In the Scenario Manager dialog box, click "Add" to create a new scenario.

5. Name the scenario and specify which cells should be changed for this scenario.

6. Enter the values for the changed cells in the "Changing Cells" field.

7. Click "OK" to add the scenario.

8. You can create multiple scenarios by repeating steps 4 to 7, each with different assumptions.

9. To switch between scenarios, go back to the Scenario Manager dialog box, select the scenario you want to view, and click "Show."

Scenario Manager is valuable for analyzing how different sets of assumptions impact your model's outcomes. It's commonly used in financial planning to assess the effects of various market conditions or business strategies.

Data Tables

Data Tables in Excel allow you to perform sensitivity analysis by automatically calculating and displaying a range of possible outcomes based on different input values. There are two types of Data Tables: one-variable and two-variable.

One-Variable Data Table

A one-variable Data Table helps you analyze the impact of changing a single input variable on one or more calculated results. To create a one-variable Data Table:

1. Set up a column or row with different values for the input variable you want to change.

2. In a cell, enter a formula that references the calculated result you want to observe (e.g., profit, NPV).

3. Select the range of input values and the cell containing the formula.

4. Go to the "Data" tab and click on "What-If Analysis," then select "Data Table."

5. In the Data Table dialog box, specify the cell that contains the input value you're changing.

6. Excel will generate a table displaying the calculated results for each input value.

One-variable Data Tables are useful for understanding how a single variable affects your model's outcomes, making them valuable for sensitivity analysis.

Two-Variable Data Table

A two-variable Data Table extends the concept to analyze the impact of changing two input variables simultaneously. To create a two-variable Data Table:

1. Set up a grid with different values for two input variables.

2. In a cell, enter a formula that references the calculated result you want to observe.

3. Select the range of input values for both variables and the cell containing the formula.

4. Go to the "Data" tab and click on "What-If Analysis," then select "Data Table."

5. In the Data Table dialog box, specify the cells containing the two input values.

6. Excel will generate a table displaying the calculated results for each combination of input values.

Two-variable Data Tables are particularly helpful for understanding the interactions between two variables and their combined impact on your model's outcomes.

Solver is an advanced Excel tool used for optimization and finding the optimal solution to a problem by adjusting multiple input variables. While it's commonly used in finance and operations research, it can be applied to various scenarios. Here's how to use Solver:

1. Define your objective function, which is a formula that calculates the value you want to maximize, minimize, or reach a specific target.

2. Specify the variables that can be adjusted to achieve your objective.

3. Set constraints on variables to define limitations or boundaries.

4. Access Solver by going to the "Data" tab and clicking on "Solver" in the "Analysis" group.

5. In the Solver Parameters dialog box, configure the objective, variables, constraints, and options.

6. Click "Solve," and Solver will find the optimal solution that meets your criteria.

Solver is a versatile tool for solving complex optimization problems, such as resource allocation, financial portfolio optimization, and production scheduling.

Using "What-If" Analysis for Informed Decision-Making

In conclusion, Excel's "What-If" analysis tools, including Goal Seek, Scenario Manager, Data Tables, and Solver, empower users to explore scenarios, analyze sensitivity, and optimize solutions. These tools are invaluable for making informed decisions in various domains and industries, providing a data-driven approach to problem-solving and planning. Whether you need to perform financial modeling, assess the impact of changing variables, or find the best solution to a complex problem, Excel's "What-If" analysis tools are at your disposal.

Chapter 11: Creative PowerPoint Presentations

Chapter 11: Creative PowerPoint Presentations

Section 11.1: Storytelling Through Slides

In the world of presentations, storytelling is a powerful tool. It allows you to engage your audience, convey information effectively, and leave a lasting impression. PowerPoint, as a versatile presentation software, provides numerous features and techniques to help you tell compelling stories through your slides.

The Importance of Storytelling

Before we dive into the technical aspects of PowerPoint, let's understand why storytelling is crucial in presentations. Stories are inherently captivating, and they have been a primary means of communication throughout human history. When you incorporate storytelling into your presentations, you create an emotional connection with your audience, making your message more relatable and memorable.

Structuring Your Narrative

Effective storytelling in PowerPoint begins with a well-structured narrative. Your presentation should have a clear beginning, middle, and end. Start by introducing the context or the problem you're addressing. Then, develop your story by providing information, examples, or anecdotes. Finally, conclude with a resolution or a call to action.

Visual Storytelling

Incorporating visuals into your presentation is essential for storytelling. PowerPoint allows you to add images, charts, graphs, and videos to enhance your narrative. Use visuals to illustrate your points, evoke emotions, or simplify complex concepts. Remember that a picture is worth a thousand words, and the right visual can convey your message more effectively than text alone.

Using Slide Transitions

Slide transitions are another tool at your disposal for storytelling. Instead of simply switching from one slide to the next, consider how you can use transitions to create a sense of progression in your story. Use subtle transitions to build anticipation or more dramatic ones for turning points in your narrative.

Animations for Emphasis

Animations can be used to emphasize key points in your story. You can animate text, images, or other objects to appear or disappear at specific moments. Be mindful not to overdo it, as excessive animations can distract from your message. Use animations strategically to guide your audience's attention.

Interactive Elements

For an engaging storytelling experience, consider adding interactive elements to your slides. PowerPoint offers features like hyperlinks, action buttons, and navigation menus that allow you to create interactive branching paths. This can be particularly useful for choose-your-own-adventure-style presentations or scenarios where you want the audience to participate.

Rehearsing and Timing

Storytelling requires practice, especially when it comes to timing. Rehearse your presentation multiple times to ensure that your narrative flows smoothly, and you don't rush through or linger too long on a particular point. Use PowerPoint's rehearse timings feature to synchronize your storytelling with slide transitions and animations.

Storytelling Resources

To become a better storyteller in PowerPoint, you can explore various resources, such as books, online courses, or workshops on storytelling techniques. Additionally, studying well-crafted presentations by others can provide valuable insights and inspiration.

In this section, we've touched on the fundamentals of storytelling through PowerPoint presentations. As you continue to develop your skills, you'll find that storytelling enhances your ability to inform, persuade, and engage your audience effectively. Whether you're delivering a business proposal, a sales pitch, or an educational lecture, mastering the art of storytelling in PowerPoint will set you apart as a compelling presenter.

Section 11.2: Advanced Animation and Transition Techniques

PowerPoint offers a wide range of animation and transition options that allow you to create dynamic and visually engaging presentations. In this section, we will explore advanced animation techniques to take your PowerPoint slides to the next level.

Custom Animation Sequences

Custom animation sequences give you precise control over how objects on your slides appear, disappear, and move. To apply custom animations:

1. Select the object you want to animate.
2. Navigate to the "Animations" tab on the PowerPoint ribbon.
3. Click on "Add Animation" to choose an animation effect.
4. Use the "Animation Pane" to adjust the sequence and timing of animations.

You can combine multiple animation effects on a single object and synchronize them for complex animations. Custom animations are particularly useful for highlighting specific points or guiding the audience's attention.

Motion Paths

Motion paths allow you to define a specific trajectory for an object's movement on the slide. You can create custom motion paths by:

1. Selecting the object you want to animate.
2. Going to the "Animations" tab and clicking on "Add Animation."
3. Choose "More Motion Paths" to create a custom path.

You can drag the path's endpoints to adjust the motion's direction and length. Motion paths are great for simulating movement, such as objects flying in, bouncing, or following a curved path.

Emphasis and Exit Animations

In addition to entrance animations, PowerPoint provides emphasis and exit animations. Emphasis animations can draw attention to an object already on the slide, such as making text bold or enlarging an image briefly. Exit animations determine how objects leave the slide, allowing for creative ways to transition between slides or emphasize a point.

Animation Triggers

Animation triggers allow you to control when an animation occurs, linking it to a specific event. For example, you can set an animation to trigger when a certain object is clicked or when the presenter advances to a specific slide. To set animation triggers:

1. Select the object with the animation.
2. Access the "Animation Pane."
3. Click on "Trigger" and choose the trigger object or event.

This feature adds interactivity to your presentation, allowing the audience to control the pacing of animations.

Advanced Transition Effects

PowerPoint offers numerous transition effects to smoothly move from one slide to another. While simple transitions like fades and slides are common, advanced transitions can enhance your presentation. Some advanced transition options include:

- **3D transitions:** These create a three-dimensional effect during slide transitions.
- **Morph transitions:** Morphing can animate complex changes, such as transforming one shape into another seamlessly.
- **Zoom transitions:** Zooming in or out of slides can add a cinematic feel to your presentation.

To apply advanced transitions, go to the "Transitions" tab on the PowerPoint ribbon and explore the available options.

Timing and Duration

Timing is crucial when using advanced animations and transitions. Practice your presentation to ensure that animations and transitions align with your narration. Use the "Animation Pane" and "Transition Pane" to adjust timing and duration for each element.

Remember that subtlety is key with advanced animations and transitions. Overusing them can be distracting and detract from your message. Use them sparingly to enhance specific points or create visual interest.

In conclusion, mastering advanced animation and transition techniques in PowerPoint can elevate your presentations from ordinary to extraordinary. These features enable you to engage your audience, emphasize key points, and create visually stunning effects that leave a lasting impression. Experiment with different effects and find the right balance to enhance your storytelling and message delivery.

Section 11.3: Utilizing Master Slides for Consistency

Master slides are a powerful feature in PowerPoint that allows you to maintain consistency and uniformity throughout your presentation. By creating and customizing master slides, you can control the overall layout, design, and elements that appear on every slide in your presentation. This section will explore how to utilize master slides effectively.

Understanding Master Slides

In PowerPoint, every presentation has at least one master slide, which serves as the template for all other slides. By modifying the master slide, you can make global changes that apply to all slides based on that master. Here's how to access and work with master slides:

1. Go to the "View" tab on the PowerPoint ribbon.
2. Click on "Slide Master" to access the master slides.

Customizing Master Slides

Once you're in the Slide Master view, you can make various customizations:

1. **Background:** Change the background color or add a watermark to all slides.
2. **Fonts and Styles:** Modify fonts, font sizes, and paragraph styles for headings and body text.
3. **Logos and Branding:** Add logos, corporate branding, or consistent graphic elements.
4. **Footer and Page Numbers:** Include a footer with copyright information, date, and page numbers.

5. **Slide Layouts:** Customize the layouts available for your slides, including title slides, content slides, and more.

Slide Layouts

Slide layouts are an integral part of master slides. Each layout defines the arrangement of placeholders for text, images, and other content on a slide. By customizing slide layouts in the master slide view, you ensure that all slides created based on those layouts maintain a consistent appearance. Here's how to customize slide layouts:

1. In Slide Master view, select the slide layout you want to customize.
2. Make changes to the placeholders, fonts, colors, or any other elements.
3. These changes will be applied to all slides using that layout.

Preserving Content vs. Master Slide Elements

When customizing master slides, it's important to distinguish between elements that should be consistent across all slides and those that should be unique to individual slides. Elements like titles, logos, and backgrounds are typically part of the master slide, while slide-specific content like text and images should be added to individual slides.

Using Multiple Master Slides

PowerPoint allows you to create multiple master slides within a single presentation. This is useful when you have different sections or themes in your presentation and want to maintain distinct styles. To create additional master slides:

1. In Slide Master view, go to the "Slide Master" tab.
2. Click "Insert Slide Master" to add a new one.
3. Customize the new master slide as needed.

Applying Master Slides

To apply a master slide to individual slides in your presentation:

1. Return to the normal view by clicking "Normal" on the View tab.
2. Select the slide you want to apply the master slide to.
3. Go to the "Slide Master" tab and choose the desired master slide from the "Master Layout" dropdown.

Master Slides for Consistency

Utilizing master slides ensures that your presentation maintains a consistent and professional look. It saves time by allowing you to make changes globally rather than on each slide individually. Whether you're creating a business presentation, a lecture, or a conference talk, mastering the use of master slides is essential for achieving a polished and cohesive presentation design.

Section 11.4: Embedding Video and Audio

Incorporating multimedia elements like videos and audio clips into your PowerPoint presentation can enhance your message, engage your audience, and make your presentation more dynamic. This section explores how to embed and customize videos and audio in your slides effectively.

Embedding Videos

To embed a video in your PowerPoint presentation, follow these steps:

1. Go to the slide where you want to insert the video.

2. Click on the "Insert" tab in the PowerPoint ribbon.

3. Select "Video" and choose one of the following options:

    - "Online Video" to insert a video from a website like YouTube.
    - "Video on My PC" to insert a video file stored on your computer.
    - "Video on OneDrive" to insert a video from your OneDrive account.
    - "Video from a File" to browse and select a video file from your local storage.
4. Follow the on-screen instructions to insert the video.

Once the video is inserted, you can resize and reposition it on the slide. PowerPoint provides options to play the video automatically when the slide appears or when you click it.

Video Playback Options

PowerPoint offers several video playback options:

- **Start:** Choose when the video should start playing (automatically or when clicked).
- **Trim Video:** Trim the video's beginning and end to include only the desired portion.
- **Play in Full Screen:** Enable full-screen mode when the video is played.
- **Video Styles:** Apply predefined styles to the video, such as borders and shadows.
- **Video Format:** Adjust video settings like brightness, contrast, and saturation.

Embedding Audio

To add audio to your PowerPoint presentation, follow these steps:

1. Go to the slide where you want to insert audio.

2. Click on the "Insert" tab in the PowerPoint ribbon.

3. Select "Audio" and choose one of the following options:

    - "Audio on My PC" to insert an audio file from your computer.

- "Audio on OneDrive" to insert an audio file from your OneDrive account.
- "Online Audio" to search for and insert audio from online sources like Office.com.
4. Insert the selected audio file onto the slide.

After inserting audio, you can customize its playback options, such as whether it plays automatically, when clicked, or in a loop. You can also set the audio to fade in or out and adjust its volume.

Managing Multimedia Files

It's important to keep your multimedia files organized. PowerPoint allows you to embed videos and audio directly into your presentation, which means that the files become part of the presentation file. However, this can increase the file size significantly.

To manage multimedia files:

1. Ensure that video and audio files are in a suitable format (e.g., MP4 for videos, MP3 for audio) and appropriately compressed to reduce file size.
2. Consider using cloud storage services like OneDrive to host larger multimedia files and insert them from there.
3. Be cautious when sharing presentations with embedded multimedia elements, as the recipient may need the correct software or codecs to play them.

Testing Playback

Before your actual presentation, it's essential to test the playback of embedded videos and audio. Different computers and venues may have varying configurations and software versions that can affect multimedia playback. Rehearse your presentation on the equipment you'll be using to ensure a seamless experience during your actual presentation.

Enhancing Engagement

Embedding video and audio elements into your PowerPoint presentation can significantly enhance engagement and make complex topics more accessible. Whether you're illustrating a concept, showcasing a product, or adding a musical touch to your slides, the effective use of multimedia can captivate your audience and deliver a memorable presentation.

Section 11.5: Interactive Presentations and Audience Engagement

Engaging your audience and keeping them actively involved during your PowerPoint presentation can make the difference between a memorable talk and a forgettable one. In this section, we'll explore various techniques and strategies for creating interactive presentations that capture your audience's attention and participation.

1. Polls and Surveys

Integrating live polls and surveys into your presentation can instantly involve your audience. Tools like Microsoft Forms or third-party polling software can be used to collect real-time feedback or gauge the audience's opinions. You can display the results on your slides to spark discussions or provide insights.

2. Interactive Quizzes

Create interactive quizzes related to your presentation's content. These quizzes can be presented at specific intervals, encouraging active participation and testing the audience's understanding. You can use tools like Microsoft Forms, Mentimeter, or dedicated quiz software to build and display quizzes within your slides.

3. Live Demonstrations

Whenever possible, include live demonstrations to illustrate your points. For instance, if you're presenting a software product, showcase its features interactively. Live demos can create a sense of participation as the audience sees the product in action.

4. Q&A Sessions

Incorporate designated question-and-answer (Q&A) sessions throughout your presentation. Encourage your audience to ask questions or provide comments. You can allocate time for Q&A after each major section or at the end of your presentation. Addressing questions directly fosters engagement and demonstrates your expertise.

5. Group Activities

Break your audience into smaller groups for discussions or activities related to your presentation topic. Afterward, each group can share their findings or insights with the larger audience. This approach promotes collaboration and allows attendees to actively contribute.

6. Interactive Storytelling

Craft your presentation as a narrative that unfolds interactively. Pose questions or scenarios to the audience and involve them in decision-making processes within the story. This technique can create suspense and engagement as attendees anticipate the story's outcome.

7. Audience Response Systems

Consider using audience response systems or clickers, which allow attendees to provide instant feedback or responses to your questions. These systems can aggregate and display responses in real time, adding an element of excitement as the audience sees their collective input.

8. Gamification

Incorporate elements of gamification into your presentation. Create challenges, quizzes, or competitions with rewards or recognition for participants who excel. Gamification can make your presentation more enjoyable and competitive, driving engagement.

9. Social Media Interaction

Encourage your audience to share thoughts, questions, or feedback on social media platforms during your presentation using a designated hashtag. Display selected social media posts on your slides to showcase the online conversation and encourage participation.

10. Augmented Reality (AR) and Virtual Reality (VR)

For advanced presentations, consider leveraging AR and VR technologies. These immersive experiences can transport your audience to different environments or scenarios, allowing them to interact with content in unique ways.

Remember that the choice of interactive elements should align with your presentation's goals and your audience's preferences. Overloading your slides with too many interactive components can be distracting, so strike a balance that enhances your message while keeping your audience engaged and informed.

Chapter 12: Outlook's Advanced Features

In this chapter, we delve into the advanced features and functionalities of Microsoft Outlook, an indispensable tool for managing emails, calendars, and tasks. Whether you're a seasoned Outlook user or looking to harness its full potential, this chapter will explore the intricacies and capabilities that can enhance your email communication and productivity.

Section 12.1: Custom Rules and Alerts

Outlook's ability to automate email management tasks through custom rules and alerts can significantly streamline your email workflow. Custom rules allow you to define specific actions that Outlook should take when incoming messages meet certain criteria. Alerts, on the other hand, provide visual and auditory notifications for important messages or events. Let's explore these features in detail:

Creating Custom Rules

Custom rules are powerful tools for automating repetitive email actions. Here's how to create and manage them:

1. **Open Outlook:** Launch Microsoft Outlook and ensure you're in the inbox or folder where you want to apply the rule.

2. **Go to the Home Tab:** Click on the "Home" tab in the Outlook ribbon.

3. **Select "Rules":** In the "Move" group, click on "Rules" and then select "Manage Rules & Alerts."

4. **Create a New Rule:** In the "Rules and Alerts" dialog box, click on "New Rule."

5. **Choose a Template or Start from Scratch:** Outlook provides rule templates for common tasks, or you can create a custom rule from scratch. Choose the option that suits your needs.

6. **Set Conditions:** Define the conditions that incoming messages must meet for the rule to apply. For example, you can specify criteria like sender, subject, or keywords.

7. **Specify Actions:** Determine the action(s) Outlook should take when a message meets the defined conditions. Actions can include moving messages to specific folders, flagging messages, forwarding messages, or assigning categories.

8. **Exceptions (Optional):** You can add exceptions to rules to further refine their behavior. For instance, you might want a rule to apply to all emails except those from a particular sender.

9. **Name Your Rule:** Give your rule a descriptive name to easily identify its purpose.

10. **Apply the Rule:** Choose whether to apply the rule to messages already in your inbox and whether to run the rule automatically.

11. **Finish and Apply:** Review your rule settings and click "Finish" to create the rule. Click "Apply" to apply the rule immediately to your inbox.

Managing Rules

After creating rules, you can manage and edit them as needed:

1. **Open the Rules and Alerts Dialog:** Access the "Rules and Alerts" dialog as explained earlier.

2. **Select the Rule:** In the "E-mail Rules" tab, select the rule you want to modify or delete.

3. **Edit or Delete Rule:** Click on "Change Rule" to modify the rule's conditions or actions. To delete a rule, click on "Delete."

4. **Apply Changes:** After editing the rule, click "Finish" to save your changes.

Creating Rules from Messages

You can also create rules directly from messages in your inbox:

1. **Right-Click the Message:** Right-click on the email message you want to create a rule for.

2. **Select "Rules":** From the context menu, choose "Create Rule."

3. **Set Conditions and Actions:** Follow the same steps as outlined above for creating rules from scratch.

Using Alerts

Outlook alerts provide visual and auditory notifications for specific messages or events. To set up alerts:

1. **Open Outlook:** Launch Outlook and go to the inbox or folder where you want to create an alert.

2. **Select the Message:** Click on the message you want to set an alert for.

3. **Go to the "Message" Tab:** In the Outlook ribbon, go to the "Message" tab.

4. **Click on "Follow Up" Dropdown:** In the "Tags" group, click on the "Follow Up" dropdown arrow.

5. **Choose "Add Reminder":** Select "Add Reminder" from the dropdown.

6. **Set Alert Options:** In the "Custom" dialog box, you can specify when and how you want to be alerted for this message.

7. **Save and Close:** Click "OK" to save your alert settings.

Custom rules and alerts in Outlook provide you with fine-grained control over your email management, helping you stay organized and ensuring that important messages are never missed. In Section 12.2, we'll explore effective email campaigns and advanced communication techniques in Outlook.

Section 12.2: Effective Email Campaigns

In this section, we will delve into the art of creating effective email campaigns using Microsoft Outlook. Email campaigns are widely used for marketing, communication, and outreach purposes. Outlook provides several features and best practices that can help you design and execute successful email campaigns.

Understanding Email Campaigns

Email campaigns involve sending a series of emails to a specific group of recipients with a common goal. Whether you are promoting a product, sharing updates, or raising awareness, well-executed email campaigns can yield excellent results. Here are the key components of a successful email campaign:

1. **Define Your Goals:** Clearly outline the objectives of your email campaign. What do you want to achieve? Common goals include increasing sales, driving traffic to a website, or building brand awareness.

2. **Segment Your Audience:** Divide your recipient list into segments based on demographics, interests, or behavior. Tailoring your emails to specific segments ensures that your message is relevant to each group.

3. **Create Compelling Content:** Craft engaging and valuable content for your emails. Use concise and persuasive language, and include compelling visuals when relevant.

4. **Choose the Right Timing:** Timing is crucial. Send your emails at times when your target audience is most likely to check their inbox. Consider time zones and cultural factors.

5. **Personalization:** Personalize your emails with recipient names and other relevant details. Personalized emails tend to perform better than generic ones.

6. **A/B Testing:** Experiment with different subject lines, content, and designs to optimize your emails. A/B testing can help you identify what resonates best with your audience.

7. **Automation:** Use email marketing tools or Outlook features like "Rules and Alerts" to automate the sending of emails. Automation saves time and ensures consistency.

8. **Monitoring and Analysis:** Track the performance of your email campaign. Monitor open rates, click-through rates, and conversion rates. Use this data to refine your future campaigns.

Creating Email Campaigns in Outlook

Outlook offers several features that can be used for creating and managing email campaigns:

1. Email Templates

Outlook allows you to create and save email templates, which are pre-designed email formats that you can reuse for your campaigns. To create a template:

1. **Compose a New Email:** Start by composing a new email in Outlook.

2. **Design Your Email:** Customize the email with the desired content, including text, images, and links.

3. **Save as Template:** After composing the email, go to the "File" menu, select "Save As," and choose "Outlook Template (.oft)." Save the template to a location of your choice.

Now, whenever you want to send an email as part of your campaign, you can use this template as a starting point, saving you time and ensuring consistency in your emails.

Outlook's mail merge feature allows you to send personalized emails to a large list of recipients. To perform a mail merge:

1. **Prepare Your Data:** Ensure that you have a spreadsheet or data source with recipient information, such as names and email addresses.

2. **Create a New Email:** Start a new email in Outlook.

3. **Go to the "Mailings" Tab:** In the email message, go to the "Mailings" tab in the Outlook ribbon.

4. **Select "Start Mail Merge":** Click on "Start Mail Merge" and choose "Email Messages."

5. **Insert Merge Fields:** Place your cursor where you want to insert personalized information (e.g., recipient's name) and select the corresponding field from your data source.

6. **Complete the Mail Merge:** Follow the prompts to complete the mail merge, specifying the data source and choosing the recipients.

7. **Send Your Campaign:** Once you've configured the mail merge, Outlook will send individualized emails to each recipient based on the data source.

3. Tracking and Reporting

Outlook allows you to request read receipts for your emails, providing insight into whether recipients have opened your messages. While not all recipients may respond to read receipt requests, this feature can help you gauge engagement to some extent. To request a read receipt:

1. **Compose Your Email:** Compose your campaign email as usual.

2. **Enable Read Receipts:** In the email composition window, go to the "Options" tab and check the "Request a Read Receipt" box.

3. **Send Your Email:** Send your campaign email. Recipients who choose to send read receipts will trigger a notification in your inbox.

Best Practices for Email Campaigns

To maximize the effectiveness of your email campaigns in Outlook, consider these best practices:

1. **Segment Your Audience:** Customize your emails for different recipient segments based on their interests or behavior.

2. **Mobile Optimization:** Ensure that your emails are mobile-friendly, as many recipients check emails on mobile devices.

3. **Clear Call to Action (CTA):** Include a compelling CTA in your emails to guide recipients on the desired action, such as making a purchase or clicking a link.

4. **Testing:**

Section 12.3: Managing Multiple Email Accounts

Managing multiple email accounts in Microsoft Outlook is a common scenario, especially for professionals and individuals who use separate email addresses for work, personal use, or various projects. Outlook provides robust features to help you efficiently manage multiple email accounts from a single interface.

Adding Additional Email Accounts

To get started with managing multiple email accounts in Outlook, you'll need to add these accounts to the application. Here's how to do it:

1. **Open Outlook:** Launch Microsoft Outlook on your computer.

2. **Access Account Settings:** Click on the "File" tab in the top-left corner of the Outlook window. Then, click on "Add Account" under the "Info" category.

3. **Enter Email Address:** In the "Add Account" window, enter the email address you want to add, and click "Next."

4. **Password and Authentication:** Outlook will prompt you for the password associated with the email account. Enter the password and click "Sign In" or "Next."

5. **Account Configuration:** Outlook will automatically configure the email account settings if it's a well-known email service provider like Microsoft 365, Gmail, or Yahoo. If not, you may need to manually enter server details, which your email provider can provide.

6. **Complete Setup:** Follow the on-screen instructions to complete the setup process. Outlook will perform a test to ensure it can connect to the email server. Once the test is successful, click "Finish."

7. **Repeat for Additional Accounts:** To add more email accounts, repeat the process. Each account you add will be listed in the left-hand navigation pane of Outlook.

Navigating Between Email Accounts

After adding multiple email accounts, you can easily navigate between them within Outlook. Here's how to switch between email accounts:

1. **Navigation Pane:** In the left-hand navigation pane of Outlook, you will see a list of all the email accounts you've added. Each account is represented by its email address or a custom name you've assigned.

2. **Click on an Account:** To switch to a different email account, simply click on the account's name or email address in the navigation pane.

3. **Access Email and Folders:** Once you've selected an account, you can access its inbox, sent items, folders, and other email-related features as if you were using that account exclusively.

Sending Emails from Different Accounts

Outlook allows you to send emails from any of the email accounts you've added. This is particularly useful when you want to maintain separate sender identities for different purposes. Here's how to send emails from different accounts:

1. **Compose a New Email:** Click on the "New Email" button in Outlook to start composing a new message.

2. **From Field:** In the new email composition window, you will see a "From" field. Click on the drop-down arrow next to it.

3. **Select an Account:** A list of your added email accounts will appear. Choose the account from which you want to send the email.

4. **Compose and Send:** Complete the email as usual, and when you're ready to send it, click the "Send" button. The email will be sent from the selected account.

Managing Emails Across Accounts

Outlook provides several tools to help you efficiently manage emails across multiple accounts:

- **Unified Inbox:** You can create a unified inbox that displays emails from all your accounts in one place. This makes it easier to view and respond to emails without switching between accounts.

- **Rules and Filters:** Outlook allows you to create rules and filters that automatically organize emails into folders or apply actions based on specific criteria. This can be particularly helpful for managing emails from different accounts.

- **Color Coding:** You can assign different colors to emails or folders associated with each account. This visual distinction makes it easier to identify emails from specific accounts at a glance.

- **Quick Access:** Use the "Favorites" section in the navigation pane to pin frequently accessed folders or accounts for quick access.

- **Notifications:** Configure email notifications so that you receive alerts for important emails in all your accounts. You can customize notification settings for each account.

Outlook uses data files (PST or OST files) to store emails, contacts, and other data associated with each account. By default, each email account has its own data file, ensuring separation of data between accounts.

It's important to be aware of the data files for each account, especially if you're using Outlook on multiple devices. Managing data files ensures that emails are synchronized correctly and that changes made on one device are reflected on others.

Conclusion

Efficiently managing multiple email accounts in Outlook is crucial for maintaining productivity and staying organized. With the ability to add, switch between, and send emails from different accounts, Outlook offers a comprehensive solution for email management across personal, professional, and project-related accounts. By utilizing features like unified inboxes, rules, and color coding, you can streamline your email workflow and ensure that you

---

Section 12.4: Data Security and Privacy in Outlook

Data security and privacy are of paramount importance when managing multiple email accounts in Microsoft Outlook. Whether you're using Outlook for personal correspondence, work-related communication, or both, it's crucial to take steps to safeguard your data and maintain your privacy. This section covers essential aspects of data security and privacy in Outlook.

Account Security

1. *Strong Passwords: Ensure that you use strong, unique passwords for each of your email accounts added to Outlook. A strong password typically includes a combination of upper and lower-case letters, numbers, and special characters. Avoid using easily guessable information like names or birthdays.*

2. *Two-Factor Authentication (2FA): Enable 2FA or multi-factor authentication (MFA) wherever possible for your email accounts. This adds an extra layer of security by requiring a second verification step, such as a code sent to your mobile device, in addition to your password.*

3. *Regular Password Changes: Periodically change your email account passwords to reduce the risk of unauthorized access. Use a password manager to help you generate and store complex passwords securely.*

4. *Account Recovery Options: Set up account recovery options, such as alternative email addresses or phone numbers, in case you ever lose access to your primary email account.*

5. *Beware of Phishing: Be cautious of phishing emails that may attempt to trick you into revealing your login credentials. Always verify the sender's identity and avoid clicking on suspicious links.*

Email Encryption

1. *Secure Sockets Layer (SSL)/Transport Layer Security (TLS): Ensure that your email accounts are configured to use SSL/TLS encryption for incoming and outgoing emails. This encryption secures the communication between your email client (Outlook) and the email server.*

2. *Email Encryption Services: Consider using email encryption services or plugins that offer end-to-end encryption. These services encrypt your emails in a way that only the intended recipient can decrypt and read them.*

3. *Digital Signatures: You can digitally sign your emails in Outlook, providing recipients with a way to verify the authenticity of the sender and ensuring that the email has not been tampered with during transit.*

Privacy Settings

1. *Email Tracking Prevention: Outlook has privacy settings that allow you to prevent senders from tracking when you've opened their emails. This can help protect your privacy and prevent unwanted tracking.*

2. *Safe and Blocked Senders: Use Outlook's "Safe Senders" and "Blocked Senders" lists to control which emails you receive. Add trusted senders to the safe list and block unwanted senders to reduce spam and phishing attempts.*

3. Data Sharing Permissions: Review and adjust the data sharing permissions in Outlook settings. Ensure that you're comfortable with the data that Outlook may collect for features like focused inbox and search suggestions.

4. Reading Pane Settings: Configure the reading pane settings to control whether email content is automatically displayed when you select an email. This can help prevent unintended exposure to potentially harmful content.

Email Archiving and Backup

1. Automatic Archiving: Outlook allows you to set up automatic email archiving, which moves older emails to a separate archive folder. This helps keep your inbox organized and reduces the risk of data loss.

2. Regular Backups: Consider regularly backing up your Outlook data files (PST or OST files) to an external location or a secure cloud storage service. This ensures that you have a copy of your emails in case of data loss or hardware failure.

Privacy Awareness

1. Email Content: Be mindful of the information you share via email, especially in a work context. Avoid sharing sensitive or confidential data unless it's necessary and secure.

2. Recipient Verification: Before sending sensitive information, verify the recipient's email address to avoid sending it to the wrong person by mistake.

3. Email Retention Policies: Understand your organization's email retention policies, if applicable. These policies dictate how long emails are stored and when they may be permanently deleted.

Regular Software Updates

Ensure that your Outlook application is up to date with the latest security patches and updates. Microsoft regularly releases updates to address security vulnerabilities and improve overall software security.

By implementing these security and privacy best practices, you can enhance the protection of your email accounts and data while using Microsoft Outlook for managing multiple email accounts. Being proactive in securing your email accounts is a fundamental step in maintaining your digital privacy and preventing unauthorized access to your sensitive information.

Section 12.5: Troubleshooting Common Outlook Issues

Microsoft Outlook is a powerful email client, but like any software, it can encounter issues from time to time. In this section, we'll explore some common problems that Outlook users may face and provide troubleshooting tips to help resolve them.

1. Outlook Crashes or Freezes

Outlook may occasionally crash or freeze, causing inconvenience. To troubleshoot:

- Check for software updates: Ensure that Outlook is up to date with the latest patches and updates.
- Disable add-ins: Some add-ins can cause stability issues. Try disabling them one by one to identify the problematic one.
- Repair Outlook: You can run the built-in Outlook Repair Tool to fix corrupted files.

2. Slow Performance

Outlook may become slow, especially with large mailboxes. To improve performance:

- Archive old emails: Move older emails to archive folders to reduce the size of your mailbox.
- Compact Data Files: Use the "Compact Now" option in Outlook's Data File Settings to optimize mailbox performance.
- Limit synchronization: Reduce the frequency of synchronization with email servers for non-essential folders.

3. Email Sending/Receiving Issues

If Outlook isn't sending or receiving emails as expected:

- Check internet connection: Ensure you have an active and stable internet connection.
- Verify server settings: Double-check email server settings, including SMTP and POP/IMAP configurations.
- Test in Safe Mode: Launch Outlook in Safe Mode to see if add-ins are causing the problem.

4. Missing or Duplicate Emails

Sometimes, emails may go missing or duplicate. To address this:

- Check Junk and Deleted folders: Emails can end up in these folders accidentally.
- Disable rules: Overly complex or conflicting email rules can cause issues. Disable or simplify rules.
- Scan for malware: Malware or viruses can affect email integrity. Run a malware scan.

5. Password or Login Issues

If you're having trouble with passwords or logging in:

- Verify password: Ensure you're using the correct password for your email account.
- Update email settings: Sometimes, server settings change. Verify and update your email account settings.
- Reset password: If needed, reset your email account password through your email provider.

6. Unresponsive Add-Ins

Add-ins can enhance Outlook but may sometimes become unresponsive:

- Disable or update add-ins: Disable or update add-ins that are not working correctly.
- Check for compatibility: Ensure add-ins are compatible with your Outlook version.

7. Profile Corruption

Profile corruption can lead to various issues. To address it:

- Create a new profile: You can create a new Outlook profile and add your email accounts to it.
- Repair Office installation: Use the Microsoft Office Repair Tool to repair any corrupted Office components.

8. Calendar or Meeting Issues

Issues related to calendars and meetings can disrupt productivity:

- Verify calendar settings: Double-check calendar settings, permissions, and sharing options.
- Re-create calendar items: For recurring issues, consider recreating problematic calendar items.

9. PST/OST File Problems

Outlook data files (PST/OST) may become corrupted:

- Repair PST/OST files: Use the "Inbox Repair Tool" (ScanPST.exe) to repair damaged data files.
- Backup regularly: Regularly back up your PST/OST files to prevent data loss.

10. Search Problems

If Outlook's search function isn't working correctly:

- Rebuild search index: Rebuilding the search index can often resolve search issues.
- Check search options: Review search options and filters to ensure they are correctly configured.

These troubleshooting tips should help you address common Outlook issues. If problems persist, consider reaching out to Microsoft Support or your organization's IT department for further assistance. Keep in mind that regular maintenance, updates, and backups are essential to keeping Outlook running smoothly.

Chapter 13: Access for Advanced Users

Section 13.1: Complex Query Design

In this section, we delve into complex query design in Microsoft Access, building upon the foundational knowledge of database queries. Complex queries allow you to retrieve specific data from one or more tables by applying multiple criteria and operators. They are essential for obtaining precise and customized information from your database.

Understanding Complex Queries

Complex queries, often referred to as multi-criteria or multi-condition queries, involve the use of logical operators, wildcards, and functions to filter, sort, and manipulate data. They can be used to answer intricate questions, perform calculations, and generate reports with detailed insights.

SQL and Query Design View

Access provides two primary methods for creating complex queries: SQL (Structured Query Language) and Query Design View. SQL allows you to write custom queries using a language understood by most relational databases. Query Design View offers a graphical interface for designing queries without writing SQL code directly.

Building Complex Criteria

To create complex queries, you'll need to understand how to build complex criteria. Here are some key components:

1. Logical Operators

Logical operators like AND, OR, and NOT are used to combine conditions in a query. For example, you can retrieve records that meet both Condition A AND Condition B.

2. Wildcards

Wildcards, such as asterisks (*) and question marks (?), allow for flexible matching in criteria. They are especially useful for pattern matching when dealing with text fields.

3. Functions

Access provides various built-in functions that can be applied to fields in queries. Functions enable data transformation, calculations, and formatting within your query.

4. Parameter Queries

Parameter queries prompt users to input values when the query is executed. This dynamic approach allows users to filter data based on their specific criteria.

Examples of Complex Queries

Let's explore a few examples of complex queries:

Example 1: Sales Analysis

Imagine you have a database with sales data. You can create a complex query to retrieve sales records for a specific date range, for a particular product category, and with sales values exceeding a certain threshold.

Example 2: Employee Database

In an employee database, you can design a complex query to find employees who meet multiple criteria, such as having a certain job title, working in a specific department, and being hired after a particular date.

Combining Criteria

When designing complex queries, it's crucial to understand how criteria are combined. The use of parentheses helps establish the order of operations. For instance, (A AND B) OR (C AND D) ensures that either A and B or C and D conditions are met.

Query Optimization

Optimizing complex queries is essential for maintaining database performance. Indexing relevant fields, minimizing the use of wildcards, and avoiding unnecessary calculations are some strategies to enhance query speed.

In summary, complex query design in Microsoft Access empowers you to extract precise data from your database by applying multiple criteria and operators. Whether you're analyzing sales data, managing employees, or conducting research, mastering complex queries is a valuable skill for advanced Access users. In the next sections, we'll delve into database security and integrity, advanced form and report design, using VBA in Access, and integrating Access with web applications to further enhance your Access expertise.

Section 13.2: Database Security and Integrity

Database security and integrity are paramount when working with Microsoft Access, especially for advanced users who handle sensitive or critical data. In this section, we'll explore the concepts, techniques, and best practices to ensure your Access databases are secure and maintain data integrity.

Understanding Database Security

Database security involves protecting your data from unauthorized access, modifications, or deletions. Access provides several mechanisms to enhance database security:

1. User-Level Security

Access allows you to implement user-level security, where you can define user accounts and control their access rights to specific tables, queries, forms, reports, and macros. By setting permissions, you can restrict who can view, edit, or delete data.

2. Password Protection

You can assign passwords to your database file or specific objects within the database. Password protection adds an additional layer of security by requiring users to enter the correct password before accessing the database.

3. Encryption

To safeguard data during transmission, you can use encryption when connecting to external data sources or using Access with Microsoft SQL Server. Encryption ensures that data remains confidential while in transit.

4. Trusted Locations

Access provides the concept of trusted locations where you can specify folders or network locations that are considered safe. Only databases from trusted locations are allowed to run code, reducing the risk of running potentially harmful macros.

Data Integrity

Data integrity refers to the accuracy and consistency of data within your database. Ensuring data integrity is crucial to maintaining the reliability of your database. Here are some key considerations:

1. Data Validation Rules

You can define validation rules for fields to ensure that data entered meets specific criteria. For example, you can set a rule to validate that dates are within a certain range or that text fields follow a particular format.

2. Referential Integrity

Referential integrity ensures that relationships between tables are maintained. Access can enforce referential integrity by preventing actions that would result in orphaned records or broken relationships.

3. Data Types

Choosing appropriate data types for your fields helps prevent data entry errors. Access provides various data types, such as Text, Number, Date/Time, and Currency, each with its own validation and formatting options.

4. Constraints and Triggers

Advanced users can implement constraints and triggers using SQL statements to enforce specific rules and actions within the database. Constraints prevent invalid data, while triggers can automate actions based on data changes.

Backup and Recovery

Regularly backing up your Access database is essential to protect against data loss due to hardware failures, corruption, or accidental deletions. Access offers built-in tools for creating database backups, and you can schedule these backups to occur automatically.

Access Security in a Network Environment

In a networked environment, additional security measures may be necessary. Firewalls, intrusion detection systems, and user authentication protocols can further enhance the security of your Access databases.

Security Updates

Finally, keeping your Access software up to date is crucial. Microsoft regularly releases security updates and patches to address vulnerabilities. Ensuring your software is current helps protect your database from potential threats.

In conclusion, database security and integrity are vital aspects of working with Microsoft Access. Whether you're managing a small business database or a large-scale application, implementing user-level security, validation rules, referential integrity, and regular backups are essential practices to safeguard your data and maintain its accuracy. In the subsequent sections, we'll explore advanced form and report design, using VBA (Visual Basic for Applications) in Access, and integrating Access with web applications to further expand your Access capabilities.

Section 13.3: Advanced Form and Report Design

In this section, we will delve into advanced form and report design techniques in Microsoft Access. Forms and reports are essential components of any database application, as they provide user-friendly interfaces for data entry, viewing, and reporting. By mastering these advanced design techniques, you can create highly customized and efficient forms and reports that meet your specific needs.

Creating Custom Forms

1. Tab Controls and Navigation Forms

Tab controls and navigation forms allow you to organize and present information in a user-friendly manner. Tab controls divide a form into multiple pages, each containing a different set of controls. Navigation forms, on the other hand, provide a centralized hub for navigating through various forms and reports within your database.

```vba
' Example of opening a form within a navigation form using VBA
DoCmd.OpenForm "MyForm", acNormal, , , acFormEdit, acWindowNormal
```

2. Subforms

Subforms enable you to display related data within a main form. This is particularly useful for displaying one-to-many relationships, where each record in the main form can have multiple related records in the subform.

```vba
' Example of setting the subform control source using VBA
Me.subformControlName.SourceObject = "MySubform"
```

3. Conditional Formatting

Conditional formatting allows you to change the appearance of form controls based on specified conditions. For instance, you can highlight overdue tasks in red or apply different formatting to positive and negative numbers.

```vba
' Example of applying conditional formatting using VBA
If Me.AmountDue > 0 Then
    Me.AmountDue.ForeColor = RGB(255, 0, 0) ' Red text for positive amounts
End If
```

4. Data Validation

Implement data validation rules to ensure that users enter accurate and consistent data. You can use expressions or VBA code to validate fields, display custom error messages, and prevent invalid data entry.

```vba
' Example of data validation using VBA
Private Sub Form_BeforeUpdate(Cancel As Integer)
    If IsNull(Me.Field1) Or Me.Field1 < 0 Then
        MsgBox "Field1 must be a positive value.", vbExclamation
        Cancel = True
    End If
End Sub
```

Designing Custom Reports

1. Grouping and Sorting

Grouping and sorting data in reports are essential for organizing information logically. You can group data by a specific field, apply sorting criteria, and create summary calculations for each group.

```vba
' Example of grouping and sorting in a report using VBA
Me.GroupLevel(0).ControlSource = "CategoryField"
Me.OrderBy = "SalesAmount DESC"
```

2. Adding Calculations

Reports often require calculations such as totals, averages, or percentages. You can add calculated fields to your reports using expressions or VBA functions.

```
' Example of adding a calculated field in a report using VBA
Me.Controls("TotalSales").ControlSource = "=Sum([SalesAmount])"
```

3. Custom Headers and Footers

Customizing report headers and footers allows you to include additional information, such as report titles, page numbers, and date stamps.

```
' Example of customizing report headers and footers using VBA
Me.PageHeaderSection.Controls("ReportTitle").Caption = "Sales Report"
Me.PageFooterSection.Controls("PageNumber").Caption = "Page " & [Page]
```

4. Interactive Reports

You can make reports interactive by adding hyperlinks or buttons that navigate to other reports or forms, enhancing the user experience.

```
' Example of creating a hyperlink in a report using VBA
Me.HyperlinkControl.HyperlinkAddress = "mailto:example@email.com"
```

Automation with VBA

For advanced form and report customization, VBA (Visual Basic for Applications) is a powerful tool. VBA allows you to automate processes, create custom functions, and respond to user interactions programmatically. It opens up endless possibilities for tailoring your Access application to your specific requirements.

In conclusion, advanced form and report design in Microsoft Access offer extensive opportunities for creating user-friendly, data-rich applications. By mastering tab controls, subforms, conditional formatting, data validation, grouping, sorting, and VBA automation, you can take your database design to the next level and provide efficient and highly customized solutions for your users. In the following sections, we will explore using VBA in Access further and integrating Access with web applications to expand your database capabilities even further.

Section 13.4: Using VBA in Access

Microsoft Access provides a powerful feature known as VBA (Visual Basic for Applications), which allows you to automate tasks, create custom functions, and enhance the functionality of your database application. In this section, we will explore how to use VBA to improve your Access database.

Getting Started with VBA

To access the VBA editor in Access, open your database and navigate to the "Database Tools" tab. Then, click on "Visual Basic" or press ALT + F11. This will open the VBA editor, where you can write, edit, and manage your VBA code.

```
' Example of a simple VBA procedure
Sub HelloWorld()
    MsgBox "Hello, World!", vbInformation, "Greetings"
End Sub
```

Event-Driven Programming

VBA in Access is often used to respond to events triggered by user actions or database operations. You can write VBA code that executes when a form is opened, a button is clicked, or a record is updated.

```
' Example of an event procedure in a form
Private Sub Form_Load()
    MsgBox "Welcome to this form!", vbInformation, "Form Loaded"
End Sub
```

Custom Functions

VBA allows you to create custom functions that can be used in queries, forms, and reports. These functions can perform calculations, manipulate data, or return specific values.

```
' Example of a custom VBA function
Function CalculateDiscount(Price As Double, DiscountRate As Double) As Double
    CalculateDiscount = Price * (1 - DiscountRate)
End Function
```

Data Manipulation with VBA

VBA is a powerful tool for manipulating data in your Access database. You can use SQL statements and VBA code to insert, update, delete, and retrieve data.

```
' Example of executing an SQL query in VBA
Dim strSQL As String
strSQL = "UPDATE Customers SET ContactName='New Contact' WHERE CustomerID=1"
DoCmd.RunSQL strSQL
```

Error Handling

Robust error handling is essential in VBA to gracefully handle unexpected issues that may arise during code execution. You can use On Error statements to catch and handle errors.

```
' Example of error handling in VBA
On Error Resume Next
DoCmd.OpenForm "NonExistentForm"
If Err.Number <> 0 Then
    MsgBox "An error occurred: " & Err.Description, vbExclamation, "Error"
```

```
End If
On Error GoTo 0 ' Reset error handling
```

The VBA editor in Access provides debugging tools to help you identify and fix issues in your code. You can set breakpoints, use the Immediate window, and step through code line by line.

```
' Example of setting a breakpoint in VBA
Sub DebugExample()
    Dim x As Integer
    x = 10
    Debug.Print x ' Set breakpoint here
    x = x * 2
    Debug.Print x
End Sub
```

Creating User-Defined Forms and Dialogs

VBA allows you to create custom forms and dialogs that interact with users. These forms can be used for data entry, confirmation messages, or custom input.

```
' Example of creating a custom dialog box in VBA
Function ShowCustomDialog() As String
    Dim strInput As String
    strInput = InputBox("Enter your name:", "Custom Dialog")
    If strInput <> "" Then
        MsgBox "Hello, " & strInput & "!", vbInformation, "Greetings"
    Else
        MsgBox "You didn't enter a name.", vbExclamation, "Error"
    End If
End Function
```

In summary, VBA is a valuable tool for enhancing the functionality and automation capabilities of your Microsoft Access database. Whether you need to create custom functions, respond to user events, manipulate data, or create user-defined forms, VBA empowers you to tailor your Access application to your specific needs. In the next section, we will explore how to integrate Access with web applications, expanding your database's reach and capabilities.

Section 13.5: Integrating Access with Web Applications

In this section, we'll delve into the integration possibilities of Microsoft Access with web applications. Integrating Access with the web can expand the reach and capabilities of your database, making it accessible from anywhere and providing opportunities for collaboration and automation.

Web Forms and Data Entry

One of the key benefits of integrating Access with web applications is the ability to create web forms for data entry. Microsoft provides a feature known as Access Web Apps, which allows you to design web forms that can be used to input and manipulate data in your Access database.

```
' Example of creating a web form in Access
Sub CreateWebForm()
    DoCmd.OpenForm "MyWebForm", acFormDS
End Sub
```

Sharing Data with SharePoint

SharePoint is a widely used platform for document management and collaboration. Access can integrate seamlessly with SharePoint, enabling you to share your database and data with others through SharePoint sites.

```
' Example of linking Access data to a SharePoint list
Sub LinkToSharePoint()
    DoCmd.TransferDatabase acLink, "SharePoint", _
        "https://yoursharepointsite.com/sites/yourlist", acTable, "AccessTabl
eName", "SharePointListName"
End Sub
```

Building Custom Web Applications

Microsoft Power Apps is a tool that allows you to create custom web and mobile applications. You can use Power Apps to build web applications that interact with your Access database, providing tailored user experiences.

```
' Example of embedding a Power App in an Access form
Sub EmbedPowerApp()
    DoCmd.OpenForm "MyAccessForm"
    Forms("MyAccessForm").Object.EmbedPowerApp "https://powerappurl.com", 800
, 600
End Sub
```

Automating Data Sync

To ensure that your web application and Access database stay synchronized, you can create scheduled tasks or use Microsoft Flow (now called Power Automate) to automate data synchronization between the two environments.

```
' Example of scheduling data synchronization
Sub ScheduleDataSync()
    ' Use Task Scheduler or a similar tool to run a script at specified inter
vals
    ' The script can perform data synchronization tasks between Access and th
e web app
End Sub
```

Access allows you to create and consume web services, enabling you to interact with external web applications and APIs. You can use web services to exchange data, automate processes, and enhance the functionality of your Access database.

```
' Example of creating a web service in Access
Function MyWebService() As String
    ' Define the web service logic here
    MyWebService = "Data retrieved from the web service"
End Function
```

Mobile Access

Integrating Access with web applications also opens up the possibility of mobile access to your database. Users can access your database through web browsers on mobile devices, providing flexibility and convenience.

```
' Example of enabling mobile access to an Access Web App
Sub EnableMobileAccess()
    ' Publish your Access Web App to a web server accessible from mobile devi
ces
End Sub
```

In conclusion, integrating Microsoft Access with web applications can transform your database into a versatile and accessible tool for data management and collaboration. Whether you're creating web forms for data entry, sharing data with SharePoint, building custom web applications, automating data synchronization, or utilizing web services, these integration options empower you to harness the full potential of your Access database in the modern, interconnected world. In the upcoming chapters, we will explore more advanced techniques for leveraging the capabilities of Microsoft Office applications.

Chapter 14: OneNote Advanced Techniques

Section 14.1: Audio and Video Notes

In this section, we'll explore advanced techniques for taking notes in Microsoft OneNote, with a focus on incorporating audio and video elements into your notes. OneNote is a versatile digital note-taking application that allows you to capture and organize information in various formats, making it an ideal tool for a wide range of purposes, including meetings, lectures, brainstorming sessions, and personal journaling.

Recording Audio Notes

OneNote provides a built-in audio recording feature that enables you to capture audio notes directly within your notebooks. To get started with audio notes:

1. Open the page where you want to insert the audio note.

2. Click on the "Insert" tab in the ribbon.

3. Select "Record Audio" from the dropdown menu.

4. A recording interface will appear. Click the red "Record" button to start recording your audio note.

5. Click the "Stop" button to end the recording when you're finished.

6. You can also add a title and description to your audio note for easy reference.

```html
<!-- Example of an audio note inserted in OneNote -->
<audio controls>
  <source src="audio_note.mp3" type="audio/mpeg">
  Your browser does not support the audio element.
</audio>
```

Embedding Audio and Video Files

In addition to recording audio notes, you can also embed existing audio and video files into your OneNote pages. This allows you to reference external media content within your notes:

1. Open the page where you want to embed audio or video.

2. Click on the location where you want to insert the media file.

3. Go to the "Insert" tab and select "File Attachment."

4. Browse for the audio or video file on your computer and select it.

5. The file will be embedded on the page, and you can play it directly from OneNote.

```
<!-- Example of an embedded video in OneNote -->
<video controls width="320" height="240">
  <source src="video_clip.mp4" type="video/mp4">
  Your browser does not support the video element.
</video>
```

Linked Audio and Video Notes

OneNote allows you to create links between your audio and video notes and the corresponding text or drawings on your page. This linking feature makes it easy to jump to specific moments in your recordings:

1. Highlight the text or drawing that corresponds to a particular point in your audio or video note.

2. Right-click the selected content and choose "Link to Audio" or "Link to Video."

3. OneNote will create a hyperlink that, when clicked, takes you directly to the associated media file.

Playback and Synchronization

OneNote provides playback controls for audio and video notes, allowing you to play, pause, rewind, and fast-forward through your recordings. You can also adjust the playback speed to suit your needs.

Additionally, OneNote can synchronize your notes with the audio or video playback. This means that as you review your notes, the playback position will be synchronized with the point in your recording where you made those notes. This feature is especially useful for revisiting key moments in lectures or meetings.

In conclusion, OneNote's advanced note-taking capabilities, including audio and video integration, make it a powerful tool for capturing and organizing multimedia-rich information. Whether you're recording lectures, annotating interviews, or enhancing your personal journal with multimedia elements, OneNote provides the flexibility and functionality to meet your needs. In the next sections of this chapter, we will explore further advanced techniques for maximizing your productivity with OneNote.

Section 14.2: Handwriting and Drawing Tools

In this section, we'll delve into the powerful handwriting and drawing tools available in Microsoft OneNote. These tools allow you to create handwritten notes, sketches, diagrams, and annotations directly on your digital notebooks, providing a versatile way to express your ideas and enhance your notes with freeform content.

Digital Ink and Pen Options

OneNote offers a variety of digital ink and pen options that cater to different preferences and writing styles. You can choose from different pen types, colors, and thicknesses to customize your writing or drawing experience.

To access the digital ink options:

1. Click on the "Draw" tab in the ribbon.

2. Select the pen type, color, and thickness from the toolbar.

3. You can also use a stylus or digital pen if you're working on a touchscreen device for a more natural writing experience.

Handwriting Recognition

OneNote includes handwriting recognition capabilities, which means it can convert your handwritten notes into typed text. This feature can be incredibly useful for creating neat, searchable notes from your handwritten content.

To convert handwriting to text:

1. Write your notes or draw your diagrams using the digital ink tools.

2. Select the handwritten content you want to convert.

3. Right-click on the selected content and choose "Ink to Text" from the context menu.

OneNote will analyze your handwritten text and convert it into typed text, making it easier to read and search.

Shapes and Drawing Tools

In addition to handwriting, OneNote provides a wide range of shapes and drawing tools to help you create diagrams, flowcharts, sketches, and more. You can access these tools from the "Shapes" and "Draw" menus in the "Insert" tab.

Here are some examples of how you can use shapes and drawing tools in OneNote:

*   Create flowcharts and diagrams by connecting shapes and adding labels.
*   Draw precise geometric shapes like circles, rectangles, and triangles.
*   Add arrows, lines, and connectors to illustrate relationships.
*   Use the highlighter tool to emphasize key points or sections.

Math Equations and Formulas

OneNote also supports the input and recognition of mathematical equations and formulas. You can use the built-in math tools to write, edit, and solve equations directly within your notes.

To insert a math equation:

1. Click on the "Insert" tab.

2. Select "Equation" from the toolbar.

3. A math input panel will appear, allowing you to write or type your equation.

4. Once you've entered your equation, OneNote can help you solve it or plot graphs if needed.

Collaboration with Handwritten Content

Collaboration is made easier with OneNote's ability to share handwritten and drawn content. You can collaborate in real-time with others by sharing your notebooks via OneDrive or a shared network location. Multiple users can contribute to the same notebook, making it a valuable tool for brainstorming sessions, team meetings, or collaborative projects.

In summary, OneNote's handwriting and drawing tools offer a versatile platform for expressing ideas, creating diagrams, and annotating your digital notebooks. Whether you prefer the feel of handwritten notes or need to illustrate complex concepts, OneNote's digital ink capabilities provide a flexible and intuitive solution for capturing your thoughts and collaborating with others.

Section 14.3: Using Tags and Templates Effectively

In this section, we'll explore how to use tags and templates effectively in Microsoft OneNote. Tags and templates are powerful features that can help you organize your notes, highlight important information, and streamline your note-taking process.

Tags for Note Organization

OneNote allows you to tag specific content within your notes, making it easy to categorize, search, and filter your notes based on their content. Tags can represent different categories, priorities, or action items, and they are highly customizable to suit your needs.

To apply tags to your notes:

1. Select the content you want to tag within a note.

2. Go to the "Home" tab in the ribbon.

3. Click on the "Tags" dropdown menu to choose from a variety of predefined tags or create custom tags.

4. Once applied, tagged content can be easily identified by the tag icon next to it.

5. You can filter your notes by tags using the "Find Tags" option, allowing you to quickly access all notes related to a specific tag.

To-Do Lists and Task Management

One of the most practical uses of tags in OneNote is for creating to-do lists and managing tasks. By tagging items as tasks, you can easily track and prioritize your action items. The "To-Do" tag is a commonly used tag for this purpose.

To create a to-do list:

1. Write down your tasks or action items within your notes.

2. Select each task or action item.

3. Apply the "To-Do" tag to mark it as a task.

4. Use the "Find Tags" feature to view all your tasks in one place and check them off as you complete them.

You can also customize your to-do tags with additional information, such as due dates or priorities, by editing the tag properties.

Customizing Tags

OneNote provides the flexibility to customize and create your own tags to match your specific note-taking needs. To create custom tags:

1. Click on the "Tags" dropdown menu.

2. Select "Customize Tags" to open the "Tag Customization" dialog.

3. Click on "New Tag" to create a new custom tag.

4. Enter a name for the tag and choose an icon to represent it.

5. You can also set a keyboard shortcut for quick tagging.

6. Once created, your custom tag will appear in the "Tags" dropdown menu for easy access.

Templates for Consistency

Templates are pre-designed note layouts that you can use to maintain consistency in your notes. OneNote offers a variety of built-in templates for different purposes, such as meeting notes, project planning, and personal journals.

To apply a template to a page:

1. Go to the "Insert" tab in the ribbon.

2. Select "Page Templates" to view the available templates.

3. Choose a template that suits your needs.

4. The selected template will be applied to your current page, providing a structured layout for your content.

You can also create your own custom templates or modify existing ones to match your preferences.

Collaborative Note-Taking

Tags and templates in OneNote enhance collaborative note-taking by providing a standardized way to organize and structure content. When working on group projects or sharing notes with colleagues, using consistent tags and templates ensures that everyone can easily follow the content and action items within the notes.

In summary, leveraging tags and templates effectively in Microsoft OneNote can significantly improve your note organization, task management, and collaborative note-taking. Whether you're using tags to highlight key points or templates to maintain a consistent structure, these features enhance the versatility and productivity of your note-taking experience.

Section 14.4: Sharing and Collaborating on a Large Scale

Microsoft OneNote offers robust features for sharing and collaborating on your notes, making it an excellent tool for teamwork and large-scale projects. In this section, we will explore the various ways you can share your OneNote notebooks and collaborate with others effectively.

Sharing Notebooks

Sharing your OneNote notebooks with others is a fundamental aspect of collaboration. You can share your notebooks with colleagues, team members, or friends, allowing them to view and edit the content in real-time. Here's how to share a notebook:

1. Open the notebook you want to share in OneNote.

2. Click on the "Share" button in the upper-right corner of the application.

3. Choose whether you want to share the notebook with specific people or create a sharing link.

4. If you select "Specific People," enter the email addresses of the individuals you want to share with and set their permissions (view only or edit).

5. If you choose to create a sharing link, you can set permissions for anyone with the link, such as view-only or editing access.

6. Once shared, collaborators can access the notebook through their OneDrive or OneNote Online accounts.

Real-Time Collaboration

OneNote excels in real-time collaboration, allowing multiple users to work on the same notebook simultaneously. This feature is particularly valuable for brainstorming sessions, project planning, or team meetings. Here's how real-time collaboration works:

1. When collaborators open the shared notebook, they can see who else is working on it.

2. Changes made by one user are immediately reflected for others, ensuring that everyone is always up-to-date.

3. Collaborators can leave comments, highlight content, or insert new information in real-time.

4. The collaborative environment fosters communication and creativity, making it an ideal tool for group work.

Version History and Backup

To maintain data integrity and keep track of changes, OneNote offers version history and backup options. You can view the history of changes made to a notebook and restore previous versions if needed. This is particularly useful to recover accidentally deleted content or to review the evolution of your notes.

To access version history:

1. Right-click on the notebook in OneNote and select "Version History."

2. You can see a list of previous versions with timestamps and user details.

3. Select a version to view or restore.

OneNote also provides backup options to ensure your notes are safe. By syncing your notebooks to OneDrive or SharePoint, you create an automatic backup that can be accessed from any device.

Collaborative Note-Taking

Collaborative note-taking extends beyond sharing and editing. OneNote enables users to co-author notes during meetings or lectures. Multiple users can contribute their insights simultaneously, which is incredibly valuable for capturing diverse perspectives and ensuring comprehensive documentation.

To start collaborative note-taking:

1. Open a notebook and create a new page.

2. Click on the "Share" button in the upper-right corner of the page.

3. Invite collaborators to join the session.

4. As participants join, you can all contribute to the same page in real-time.

This feature is particularly useful for educational settings, research projects, and collaborative work environments.

Integration with Microsoft Teams

For organizations using Microsoft Teams for communication and collaboration, OneNote seamlessly integrates with Teams channels. You can create shared notebooks directly within Teams channels, making it easy to access and collaborate on notes related to specific projects or teams.

To integrate OneNote with Teams:

1. Open a Teams channel where you want to use OneNote.

2. Click on the "+" button to add a tab to the channel.

3. Select "OneNote" as the tab type and choose a notebook to link or create a new one.

4. Collaborators can access the shared notebook within the Teams channel and work together on notes.

In conclusion, Microsoft OneNote offers a rich set of features for sharing and collaborating on notes at a large scale. Whether you need to work together on projects, conduct real-time collaborative note-taking, or integrate with other Microsoft tools like Teams, OneNote provides the flexibility and functionality to enhance teamwork and productivity.

Section 14.5: OneNote for Research and Project Management

Microsoft OneNote is a versatile tool that extends its usefulness beyond simple note-taking. In this section, we will explore how you can leverage OneNote for research and project management. Whether you're a student conducting academic research or a professional managing complex projects, OneNote offers valuable features to streamline your work.

Research and Data Organization

OneNote provides a structured environment for organizing research materials, making it a powerful tool for students, academics, and researchers. Here's how you can use it effectively:

1. **Notebook Organization:** Create a dedicated notebook for your research project. Within this notebook, create sections for different aspects of your research, such as literature review, data collection, and analysis.

2. **Pages and Subpages:** Each section can contain multiple pages and subpages. Use these to organize your notes, ideas, and research findings. You can easily drag and drop pages to reorder them.

3. **Templates:** OneNote offers templates for various purposes, including research notes, project plans, and meeting agendas. Customize these templates to suit your specific needs.

4. **Tags and Labels:** Utilize OneNote's tagging feature to categorize and label important information. You can create custom tags to mark key findings, questions, or action items.

5. **Clip Web Content:** Use the OneNote Web Clipper browser extension to capture web articles, research papers, and other online content. You can annotate these clippings and organize them within your notebook.

6. **Insert Files and Attachments:** OneNote allows you to insert files and attachments directly into your notes. This is handy for including PDFs, spreadsheets, images, or any other relevant materials.

7. **Audio and Video Notes:** Record audio or video notes during research interviews, meetings, or fieldwork. These multimedia notes can be synced with your written notes for comprehensive documentation.

Project Management and Planning

OneNote's flexibility makes it an excellent choice for managing projects of all sizes. Whether you're coordinating a team effort or organizing your personal tasks, consider these project management strategies:

1. **Project Notebook:** Create a separate notebook for each project you're managing. This keeps all project-related information in one place, making it easy to access and share.

2. **Sections and Pages:** Use sections to divide your notebook into project phases or categories. Each section can contain pages dedicated to specific tasks, milestones, or project documentation.

3. **To-Do Lists:** OneNote allows you to create to-do lists within your notes. Assign tasks, set due dates, and mark items as complete. You can even tag tasks for better organization.

4. **Meeting Notes:** Record meeting minutes, agendas, and action items within OneNote. You can also share these notes with meeting attendees for transparency and accountability.

5. **Gantt Charts:** While OneNote doesn't provide Gantt chart functionality itself, you can embed Gantt charts created in other project management tools, such as Microsoft Project or Trello.

6. **Linking and Cross-Referencing:** OneNote enables you to create hyperlinks between notes and even to external websites or documents. This is useful for referencing related project materials.

7. **Collaboration:** As mentioned in previous sections, OneNote supports real-time collaboration. Team members can edit project plans, update task lists, and add comments simultaneously.

Integration with Other Tools

To enhance your research and project management workflow, consider integrating OneNote with other Microsoft and third-party tools:

1. **Microsoft Teams:** If you're working in a team, integrate your project notebook with a Microsoft Teams channel. This allows for seamless communication and collaboration.

2. **Outlook:** You can send emails to OneNote, creating a central repository for project-related correspondence. Additionally, use Outlook's calendar integration for project scheduling.

3. **Microsoft Planner:** For detailed project task management and tracking, consider using Microsoft Planner alongside OneNote. Planner offers features like Kanban boards and progress tracking.

4. **Third-Party Apps:** Explore third-party integrations that connect OneNote with project management apps like Asana, Trello, or Evernote, depending on your preferences.

In conclusion, Microsoft OneNote is a versatile tool that can significantly aid research and project management efforts. Its organizational features, collaboration capabilities, and integration options make it a valuable asset for individuals and teams seeking efficient and effective ways to handle research projects and manage tasks and projects.

Chapter 15: Office Automation and Customization

Section 15.1: Introduction to Office VBA

Visual Basic for Applications (VBA) is a powerful scripting language that allows you to automate tasks and customize Microsoft Office applications. In this section, we'll introduce you to the world of Office VBA and show you how it can enhance your productivity by automating repetitive tasks and extending the capabilities of your Office applications.

What Is VBA?

Visual Basic for Applications (VBA) is a programming language developed by Microsoft. It is embedded within Microsoft Office applications like Word, Excel, PowerPoint, and Access. VBA allows you to write custom macros and scripts to automate tasks, perform complex calculations, and interact with Office applications programmatically.

VBA is particularly useful when you find yourself repeatedly performing the same series of actions in Office applications. Instead of manually executing these tasks every time, you can write VBA code to do the work for you.

Enabling the Developer Tab

Before you can start using VBA, you'll need to enable the Developer tab in your Office applications. Here's how to do it:

1. **Microsoft Word:**

   - Click on "File" in the ribbon.
   - Select "Options."
   - In the Word Options dialog, choose "Customize Ribbon."
   - Check the "Developer" option in the right column.
   - Click "OK" to enable the Developer tab.

2. **Microsoft Excel:**

   - Click on "File" in the ribbon.
   - Select "Options."
   - In the Excel Options dialog, choose "Customize Ribbon."
   - Check the "Developer" option in the right column.
   - Click "OK" to enable the Developer tab.

3. **Microsoft PowerPoint:**

   - Click on "File" in the ribbon.
   - Select "Options."
   - In the PowerPoint Options dialog, choose "Customize Ribbon."
   - Check the "Developer" option in the right column.
   - Click "OK" to enable the Developer tab.

4. **Microsoft Access:**

    – The Developer tab is usually enabled by default in Access.

To write and run VBA code, you'll need to access the VBA editor. Here's how to open it in different Office applications:

1. **Microsoft Word, Excel, and PowerPoint:**

    – Click on the "Developer" tab.
    – Click "Visual Basic" in the "Code" group.

2. **Microsoft Access:**

    – In Access, you can access the VBA editor directly by pressing "Alt" + "F11."

Let's start with a simple example to get you acquainted with VBA. In this example, we'll create a VBA macro in Microsoft Excel that displays a message box when a button is clicked.

1. Open Excel and ensure the Developer tab is enabled.

2. Click on the "Developer" tab.

3. Click "Insert" in the "Controls" group and select the "Button (ActiveX Control)" option.

4. Draw a button on your Excel worksheet.

5. Right-click the button and select "Properties."

6. In the Properties window, change the "Name" property to "btnShowMessage" and the "Caption" property to "Show Message."

7. Double-click the button to open the VBA editor.

8. In the VBA editor, write the following code:

```
Private Sub btnShowMessage_Click()
    MsgBox "Hello, VBA World!"
End Sub
```

9. Close the VBA editor.

Now, when you click the "Show Message" button on your Excel worksheet, a message box with the text "Hello, VBA World!" will appear.

This is just a simple example of what VBA can do. You can automate complex tasks, manipulate data, and customize Office applications in countless ways using VBA. In the upcoming sections, we will explore more advanced VBA techniques and demonstrate how to use it effectively in various Office applications.

Section 15.2: Creating Custom Office Macros

In this section, we'll delve deeper into Visual Basic for Applications (VBA) and explore how to create custom macros to automate tasks and streamline your workflow in Microsoft Office applications.

The Power of Custom Macros

Custom macros, also known as VBA procedures, are scripts you write to perform specific tasks in Office applications. These tasks can range from automating repetitive actions to creating complex solutions tailored to your needs. By creating custom macros, you can boost your productivity and efficiency within Office.

The VBA Environment

Before you start writing custom macros, it's essential to understand the VBA environment. Here's a brief overview:

- **Project Explorer:** Displays a hierarchical list of all open VBA projects, such as workbooks in Excel or documents in Word.

- **Code Window:** This is where you write and edit your VBA code. You'll spend most of your time here.

- **Immediate Window:** Allows you to execute VBA code statements directly and view immediate results.

- **Properties Window:** Displays properties and settings for selected objects, such as forms or controls.

Creating Your First Custom Macro

Let's begin by creating a simple custom macro in Microsoft Word that automatically applies a specific formatting style to selected text.

1. Open Microsoft Word.

2. Click on the "Developer" tab, and if it's not visible, enable it as explained in the previous section.

3. Click "Visual Basic" in the "Code" group to open the VBA editor.

4. In the VBA editor, you'll see a window labeled "Project (YourDocumentName)," where "YourDocumentName" is the name of your open Word document.

5. Right-click on "VBAProject (YourDocumentName)" and select "Insert" > "Module." This adds a new module to your document's VBA project.

6. In the module, you can start writing your custom macro. For our example, let's create a macro that applies bold formatting to selected text:

```
Sub ApplyBoldFormatting()
    If Selection.Type = wdSelectionIP Then
        MsgBox "Please select text before running this macro.", vbExclamation
, "No Text Selected"
    Else
        Selection.Font.Bold = wdToggle
    End If
End Sub
```

7. Close the VBA editor.

Now, you've created a custom macro named "ApplyBoldFormatting" that checks if text is selected in your Word document. If text is selected, it toggles the bold formatting; otherwise, it displays a message asking you to select text first.

Running Your Custom Macro

To run your custom macro in Microsoft Word:

1. Select the text you want to apply bold formatting to.

2. Click on the "Developer" tab.

3. Click "Macros" in the "Code" group to open the "Macros" dialog.

4. Select "ApplyBoldFormatting" from the list of available macros.

5. Click "Run."

Your selected text will now have bold formatting applied. This demonstrates the power of custom macros in automating specific actions within Office applications. As you become more proficient with VBA, you can create more advanced and tailored solutions to simplify your tasks.

Section 15.3: Automating Repetitive Tasks

Automation is a key benefit of using custom macros in Microsoft Office applications. In this section, we'll explore how you can use VBA to automate repetitive tasks, saving you time and reducing the potential for errors.

Before you can automate a task, it's crucial to identify which tasks are repetitive and time-consuming. These tasks may include:

- **Data Entry:** If you frequently enter the same data into Excel or Access, automation can help.

- **Formatting:** Consistently formatting documents, spreadsheets, or presentations can be automated.

- **Report Generation:** If you regularly generate similar reports, you can create macros to do this for you.

- **Email Handling:** Managing and categorizing emails in Outlook can be automated based on criteria you define.

Recording Macros

One way to automate tasks is by recording macros. This feature is available in most Office applications and allows you to record your actions as VBA code. Here's how to record a macro in Excel as an example:

1. Open Excel.

2. Click on the "View" tab.

3. In the "Macros" group, click "Record Macro."

4. Provide a name for your macro and optionally a shortcut key.

5. Choose where to store the macro (in this workbook or a new one).

6. Click "OK" to start recording.

7. Perform the actions you want to automate.

8. Click "Stop Recording" when you're done.

Excel will have recorded your actions as VBA code, which you can run whenever you need to repeat the same steps.

Writing Custom Macros

For more complex or specific tasks, you may need to write custom VBA macros from scratch. This allows you to have complete control over the automation process. Here's an example of a custom macro in Word that replaces all occurrences of a word with another:

```
Sub ReplaceWord()
    Dim FindWord As String
    Dim ReplaceWord As String
```

```
FindWord = InputBox("Enter the word to find:")
ReplaceWord = InputBox("Enter the word to replace it with:")

Selection.Find.ClearFormatting
Selection.Find.Replacement.ClearFormatting

With Selection.Find
    .Text = FindWord
    .Replacement.Text = ReplaceWord
    .Forward = True
    .Wrap = wdFindContinue
    .Format = False
    .MatchCase = False
    .MatchWholeWord = False
    .MatchWildcards = False
    .MatchSoundsLike = False
    .MatchAllWordForms = False
End With

    Selection.Find.Execute Replace:=wdReplaceAll
End Sub
```

This custom macro prompts the user to enter the word to find and the word to replace it with. It then performs a find-and-replace operation throughout the document.

Using Loops and Conditions

To automate more advanced tasks, you can use loops and conditions in your VBA code. Loops allow you to repeat actions, while conditions help you make decisions based on specific criteria. These constructs can significantly extend the capabilities of your macros.

For instance, you can use a For loop to iterate through a range of cells in Excel and perform calculations or formatting on each cell. Similarly, you can use If...Then statements to make decisions in your code, such as applying different formatting based on certain conditions.

Error Handling

When automating tasks, it's important to include error handling in your VBA code. This ensures that if unexpected issues arise, your code can handle them gracefully. Error handling can prevent crashes and provide users with informative messages when something goes wrong.

In VBA, you can use constructs like On Error Resume Next to continue executing code even if an error occurs, or On Error GoTo to specify a custom error-handling routine.

Testing and Debugging

Before deploying your automated solution, it's crucial to thoroughly test and debug your VBA code. This involves running your macros in various scenarios to ensure they perform as expected and troubleshooting any issues that arise.

The debugging tools available in the VBA editor, such as setting breakpoints, inspecting variables, and using the Immediate window, can help you identify and fix errors in your code effectively.

Automating repetitive tasks through custom macros is a powerful way to enhance your productivity and reduce errors in Microsoft Office applications. By identifying tasks that can be automated, recording macros, writing custom VBA code, and incorporating error handling and testing, you can create efficient and reliable automation solutions tailored to your needs.

Section 15.4: Customizing the Office Ribbon

The Office Ribbon is the tabbed toolbar at the top of Microsoft Office applications like Word, Excel, and PowerPoint. It provides access to various commands and features. While Microsoft provides a standard Ribbon interface, you can customize it to better suit your workflow and access frequently used commands more efficiently.

Ribbon Customization Basics

Customizing the Ribbon allows you to create your own tabs, groups, and buttons with specific commands. Here are the steps to get started with Ribbon customization:

1. **Accessing Ribbon Customization:** In most Office applications, right-click the Ribbon and select "Customize the Ribbon..." from the context menu. This opens the "Customize the Ribbon" dialog box.

2. **Creating a New Tab:** In the "Customize the Ribbon" dialog, you can create a new tab by clicking the "New Tab" button. You can also rename it.

3. **Adding Groups:** Within your custom tab, you can add groups. Groups are sections within the tab where you can place commands. To add a group, select your custom tab, click the "New Group" button, and rename it.

4. **Adding Commands:** You can add commands to your custom groups by selecting a command from the left list and clicking the "Add" button. You can also create custom macros (VBA) and add them to your Ribbon.

5. **Organizing Commands:** Use the up and down arrows on the right side of the dialog to rearrange the order of commands within your custom tab and groups.

6. **Removing Commands:** To remove a command from your custom tab, select it in the right list and click the "Remove" button.

7. **Resetting Changes:** If you want to revert to the default Ribbon, you can click the "Reset" button.

Practical Customization Examples

Customizing the Ribbon can significantly improve your workflow. Here are some practical examples of Ribbon customization:

1. Quick Access to Macros:

If you frequently use custom VBA macros, you can create a custom tab with groups for different macros. This allows you to access your macros with a single click, streamlining your tasks.

2. Frequently Used Formatting:

If you often use specific formatting options in Word or Excel, you can create a custom tab with groups dedicated to formatting text, cells, or objects. This reduces the time spent searching through menus.

3. Custom Templates:

If your organization has specific document templates, you can create a custom tab that provides easy access to these templates. This ensures consistent document creation.

4. Collaboration Tools:

For collaborative projects, you can create a custom tab with groups for sharing, reviewing, and commenting on documents. This simplifies collaboration and document management.

5. Personalized Workflows:

Tailor the Ribbon to match your unique workflow. For example, if you're a researcher, create a custom tab with groups for literature search, data analysis, and report generation.

Ribbon Customization Limitations

While Ribbon customization offers flexibility, there are some limitations to consider:

- Ribbon customization is specific to the Office application you're working in. Changes made in Word won't affect Excel or other Office apps.

- If you share documents or templates with others, they won't see your custom Ribbon. Your customizations are stored in your local profile.

- Be cautious when removing default commands or groups. You might accidentally remove something essential.

- Ribbon customization may not be available in all versions of Office or for Office 365 web applications.

Customizing the Office Ribbon empowers you to tailor your Office applications to your specific needs and preferences. Whether you want to streamline access to frequently used commands, create custom workflows, or simplify collaboration, Ribbon customization can enhance your productivity within the Office suite.

Section 15.5: Building Add-Ins for Office Applications

Microsoft Office provides a versatile platform for productivity, and you can extend its capabilities by developing add-ins. Add-ins are custom applications or features that integrate seamlessly with Office applications like Word, Excel, PowerPoint, and Outlook. They allow you to automate tasks, add new functionalities, and tailor Office to your specific needs. In this section, we'll explore the process of building add-ins for Office applications.

Types of Office Add-Ins

Before we delve into development, it's important to understand the types of Office add-ins:

1. **Task Pane Add-Ins:** These add-ins appear as custom task panes within the Office application. They often contain user interfaces (UI) and interact with the document.

2. **Content Add-Ins:** Content add-ins can insert custom content into Office documents. They can be used to embed rich media, charts, or other data.

3. **Mail Add-Ins:** Specifically designed for Outlook, these add-ins extend email functionalities, such as processing incoming emails or integrating with external services.

Building Office Add-Ins

To build Office add-ins, you typically use web technologies like HTML, CSS, and JavaScript. Here's an overview of the development process:

1. **Choose the Office Application:** Decide which Office application your add-in will target, such as Word, Excel, PowerPoint, or Outlook.

2. **Set Up Your Development Environment:** Install the necessary tools, like Visual Studio Code or Visual Studio, and the Office Add-in project templates.

3. **Create the Add-In Project:** Start a new project using the Office Add-in template. This template provides the structure and boilerplate code for your add-in.

4. **Design the User Interface:** If your add-in requires a UI, design it using HTML and CSS. Task pane add-ins typically have a custom UI that interacts with the document.

5. **Add Functionality with JavaScript:** Implement the functionality of your add-in using JavaScript. You can use libraries like Office JavaScript API to interact with Office documents and perform various tasks.

6. **Testing and Debugging:** Test your add-in in the target Office application. Most development tools offer debugging support for Office add-ins.

7. **Security Considerations:** Ensure your add-in follows security best practices, especially if it requires access to external data or services.

8. **Deployment:** Publish your add-in to the Office Store or distribute it within your organization. Office add-ins can be sideloaded for testing or local use.

Common Use Cases for Office Add-Ins

Office add-ins can address a wide range of use cases, making Office applications more efficient and tailored to your specific needs:

- **Data Integration:** Connect Office applications to external data sources and services, allowing for real-time data updates and analysis.

- **Automation:** Automate repetitive tasks, such as data entry, formatting, or report generation, by creating custom macros and scripts.

- **Content Generation:** Build add-ins that generate dynamic content, reports, or documents based on templates and user input.

- **Collaboration:** Enhance collaboration by integrating Office applications with messaging and collaboration platforms, enabling real-time communication and document sharing.

- **Custom Functions:** Create custom Excel functions using JavaScript, providing users with specialized calculations.

- **Data Visualization:** Embed interactive charts, graphs, and visualizations directly into Office documents to enhance data analysis.

Conclusion

Building add-ins for Microsoft Office applications empowers you to extend and customize these powerful tools to better align with your workflow and business needs. Whether you want to automate tasks, integrate external data, or enhance collaboration, Office add-ins provide a versatile platform for customization and innovation within the Office suite. With the right development skills and tools, you can create tailored solutions that boost your productivity and efficiency when using Office applications.

Chapter 16: Integrating Office Applications

Section 16.1: Linking Data Across Applications

In this section, we will explore the powerful capabilities of linking data across different Microsoft Office applications. Linking allows you to establish dynamic connections between data in one application and another, enabling you to create seamless workflows and update information in real-time. This integration can significantly enhance your productivity and the accuracy of your documents, spreadsheets, and presentations.

Benefits of Linking Data

Linking data across Office applications offers several advantages:

1. **Real-Time Updates**: When you link data, changes made in one application are automatically reflected in linked documents or presentations. This ensures that your information is always up-to-date.

2. **Efficiency**: Instead of manually copying and pasting data between applications, linking allows you to work more efficiently. It reduces the risk of errors and saves time.

3. **Consistency**: Linked data ensures consistency across different documents. If you update a piece of data, such as a chart or a table, in one place, it will be updated everywhere it's linked.

4. **Data Integrity**: Since the linked data is pulled directly from the source, you can maintain data integrity. There's no risk of accidentally modifying or corrupting data during the copying process.

Linking in Microsoft Word

Microsoft Word allows you to link data from other Office applications, such as Excel and PowerPoint. To do this, follow these steps:

1. **Open Word**: Launch Microsoft Word and open the document where you want to insert linked data.

2. **Insert Object**: Click on the "Insert" tab in the Ribbon and then choose "Object" from the "Text" group.

3. **Create Link**: In the "Object" dialog box, select the "Create from file" option. Browse and select the file that contains the data you want to link.

4. **Link to File**: Check the "Link to file" option at the bottom of the dialog box. This establishes a dynamic link to the source file.

5. **Display as Icon (Optional)**: If you prefer, you can choose to display the linked data as an icon within your document. This can be helpful for visual identification.

6. **Update Options**: Word provides options for how linked data should be updated. You can choose to update it automatically or manually.

7. **Insert**: Click the "OK" button to insert the linked data into your Word document.

Linking in Excel and PowerPoint

You can also link data from Excel and PowerPoint in a similar manner. The process involves using the "Paste Special" feature in these applications to create links to data from other Office programs. This is particularly useful when you have charts, tables, or slides that need to stay synchronized with data from Excel or other sources.

Updating Linked Data

Once you have linked data in your document or presentation, it's essential to understand how to update it. In Word, Excel, or PowerPoint, you can right-click on linked content and choose the "Update Link" option to refresh the data from the source.

Conclusion

Linking data across Office applications provides a powerful way to integrate information and streamline your work. Whether you're creating reports in Word that rely on Excel data, embedding PowerPoint slides into Word documents, or any other combination, knowing how to link data effectively can enhance your productivity and improve the accuracy of your documents. In the following sections, we will explore more ways to integrate and collaborate across Office applications.

Section 16.2: Embedding Excel Data in Word and PowerPoint

In this section, we will delve into the process of embedding Excel data into Microsoft Word and PowerPoint documents. Embedding allows you to insert Excel spreadsheets or charts directly into your Word documents or PowerPoint presentations, providing a seamless way to share and present data.

Why Embed Excel Data?

Embedding Excel data offers several advantages:

1. **Dynamic Content**: The embedded Excel content remains dynamic. Any changes made to the original Excel file will automatically update in the Word or PowerPoint document, ensuring that your data is always current.

2. **Data Presentation**: You can present data in a more organized and visually appealing manner. Excel charts and tables can be easily incorporated into your documents and presentations.

3. **Data Security**: Embedding ensures that your data remains within your document, which can be important for confidentiality and security reasons.

To embed an Excel spreadsheet or chart in Microsoft Word, follow these steps:

1. **Open Word**: Launch Microsoft Word and open the document where you want to embed Excel data.

2. **Insert Object**: Click on the "Insert" tab in the Ribbon and then choose "Object" from the "Text" group.

3. **Create New**: In the "Object" dialog box, select the "Create New" tab.

4. **Microsoft Excel Worksheet**: Choose "Microsoft Excel Worksheet" from the list of available object types.

5. **Insert**: Click the "OK" button to insert a new Excel worksheet into your Word document.

6. **Excel Integration**: An Excel-like interface will appear within your Word document. You can now enter data or create charts as needed.

7. **Link Excel Data (Optional)**: If you want the embedded Excel data to be linked to an external Excel file, check the "Link to file" option when inserting the object.

8. **Editing Excel Data**: To edit the embedded Excel data, double-click within the embedded object. This will open the Excel interface, where you can make changes.

9. **Resizing and Formatting**: You can resize and format the embedded Excel object just like any other element in Word.

10. **Update Linked Data**: If you've linked the embedded Excel data to an external file and there are updates, you can right-click on the embedded object and choose "Update Link" to refresh the content.

Embedding Excel data in PowerPoint follows a similar process. Here's how to do it:

1. **Open PowerPoint**: Launch Microsoft PowerPoint and open the presentation where you want to embed Excel data.

2. **Insert Object**: Go to the slide where you want to embed the Excel data. Click on the "Insert" tab in the Ribbon and then choose "Object" from the "Text" group.

3. **Create New**: In the "Object" dialog box, select the "Create New" tab.

4. **Microsoft Excel Worksheet**: Choose "Microsoft Excel Worksheet" from the list of available object types.

5. **Insert**: Click the "OK" button to insert a new Excel worksheet into your PowerPoint slide.

6. **Excel Integration**: An Excel-like interface will appear within your PowerPoint slide. You can enter data or create charts as needed.

7. **Link Excel Data (Optional)**: If you want the embedded Excel data to be linked to an external Excel file, check the "Link to file" option when inserting the object.

8. **Editing Excel Data**: To edit the embedded Excel data, double-click within the embedded object. This will open the Excel interface, where you can make changes.

9. **Resizing and Formatting**: You can resize and format the embedded Excel object just like any other element in PowerPoint.

10. **Update Linked Data**: If you've linked the embedded Excel data to an external file and there are updates, you can right-click on the embedded object and choose "Update Link" to refresh the content.

Conclusion

Embedding Excel data into Word and PowerPoint documents allows you to create dynamic, visually appealing presentations and reports. Whether you need to include complex spreadsheets, interactive charts, or data tables, embedding provides a convenient and efficient way to enhance your documents and presentations while keeping your data up-to-date. In the following sections, we will explore more ways to integrate and collaborate across Office applications.

Section 16.3: Using Access Data in Excel and Word

In this section, we will explore how to use Access data in both Microsoft Excel and Word. Microsoft Access is a powerful database management system, and integrating its data into other Office applications can be extremely valuable for creating reports, documents, and analysis.

Why Use Access Data?

Microsoft Access is an ideal tool for managing large volumes of structured data. Integrating Access data into Excel and Word allows you to:

1. **Combine Data Sources**: Access data can be combined with data from other sources, enabling comprehensive analysis and reporting.

2. **Automate Reporting**: You can automate the process of generating reports in Word or Excel by linking them to Access queries, tables, or reports.

3. **Data Integrity**: By connecting directly to an Access database, you ensure that the data is accurate and up-to-date, eliminating the need for manual data entry.

Linking Access Data to Excel

To link Access data to Excel, follow these steps:

1. **Open Excel**: Launch Microsoft Excel and open the workbook where you want to link Access data.

2. **Data Tab**: Click on the "Data" tab in the Ribbon.

3. **Get Data**: In the "Get & Transform Data" group, select "Get Data" and then choose "From Database" > "From Microsoft Access Database."

4. **Browse for Access Database**: In the "Import Data" dialog, browse for the Access database you want to connect to.

5. **Select Data Source**: Choose the table or query from the Access database that you want to link.

6. **Load Data**: Click the "Load" button to insert the data into your Excel worksheet. You can choose to load the data as a table or a pivot table.

7. **Data Refresh**: Any changes made in the Access database will be reflected in Excel. To refresh the data, go to the "Data" tab and click "Refresh All."

Embedding Access Data in Word

To embed Access data in Microsoft Word, follow these steps:

1. **Open Word**: Launch Microsoft Word and open the document where you want to embed Access data.

2. **Insert Object**: Click on the "Insert" tab in the Ribbon and then choose "Object" from the "Text" group.

3. **Create New**: In the "Object" dialog box, select the "Create New" tab.

4. **Microsoft Access Database**: Choose "Microsoft Access Database" from the list of available object types.

5. **Insert**: Click the "OK" button to insert a new Access database object into your Word document.

6. **Access Integration**: An Access-like interface will appear within your Word document. You can now interact with the Access data.

7. **Link Access Data (Optional)**: If you want the embedded Access data to be linked to an external Access database, check the "Link to file" option when inserting the object.

8. **Editing Access Data**: To edit the embedded Access data, double-click within the embedded object. This will open the Access interface, where you can make changes.

9. **Resizing and Formatting**: You can resize and format the embedded Access object just like any other element in Word.

10. **Update Linked Data**: If you've linked the embedded Access data to an external file and there are updates, you can right-click on the embedded object and choose "Update Link" to refresh the content.

Conclusion

Integrating Microsoft Access data into Excel and Word documents streamlines data analysis and reporting processes. Whether you need to create financial reports, perform data analysis, or generate documents with up-to-date information, leveraging Access data within these Office applications enhances efficiency and data accuracy. In the following sections, we will explore more ways to integrate and automate tasks across Office applications.

Section 16.4: Dynamic Document Creation with Office

In this section, we will delve into the concept of dynamic document creation using Microsoft Office applications. Dynamic documents are documents that can automatically adjust and update their content based on various factors such as data changes, user interactions, or predefined rules. This capability is particularly useful for creating reports, contracts, proposals, and other documents that require flexibility and real-time data integration.

Benefits of Dynamic Documents

Dynamic document creation offers several advantages:

1. **Efficiency**: Automation reduces the time and effort required to create and update documents.

2. **Accuracy**: Dynamic documents ensure that data is up-to-date and accurate, reducing the risk of errors.

3. **Consistency**: Templates and predefined rules ensure consistency in document formatting and content.

4. **Customization**: Users can generate customized documents from templates, tailoring them to specific needs.

5. **Real-time Data**: Dynamic documents can pull in real-time data from various sources, keeping information current.

Microsoft Word offers features for creating dynamic documents:

- **Mail Merge**: Word's Mail Merge functionality allows you to merge data from sources like Excel or Access into predefined document templates. This is useful for generating personalized letters, envelopes, or labels.

- **Fields and Formulas**: Word supports fields and formulas that can perform calculations and dynamically update content. For example, you can create a field that calculates the sum of values in a table.

- **Content Controls**: Content controls in Word enable users to input data or select predefined options. These controls can be linked to external data sources or formulas.

Dynamic Documents in Microsoft Excel

Excel is a powerful tool for dynamic document creation:

- **Templates**: Excel templates allow you to create standardized, dynamic reports. Users can input data, and the template calculates results and updates charts and tables.

- **PivotTables and PivotCharts**: PivotTables and PivotCharts are dynamic tools for data analysis and reporting. They can be connected to external data sources and automatically refresh when data changes.

- **Formulas and Functions**: Excel's formulas and functions can perform complex calculations and return real-time results. They can be used to create dynamic financial reports, forecasts, and more.

Dynamic Documents Across Office Applications

Integrating Office applications allows you to create comprehensive dynamic documents:

- **Linking Data**: You can link data from Excel, Access, or other sources into Word documents or PowerPoint presentations. When the source data changes, the linked content updates.

- **Automation with VBA**: Visual Basic for Applications (VBA) enables advanced automation and dynamic document creation. VBA can be used to build custom functions, automate repetitive tasks, and generate reports.

Conclusion

Dynamic document creation is a valuable feature of Microsoft Office, enhancing productivity and ensuring the accuracy of documents. By leveraging the capabilities of Word, Excel, and other Office applications, users can streamline document creation, automate data integration, and create reports that adapt to changing information. In the next section, we will explore collaborative workflows that span across multiple Office applications.

Section 16.5: Collaborative Workflows Across Applications

In this final section of Chapter 16, we will focus on collaborative workflows that span across multiple Microsoft Office applications. Collaborative work often involves integrating data, content, and processes from various Office tools to create a seamless and efficient workflow. This section will explore some common scenarios and techniques for achieving effective collaboration within the Office ecosystem.

Benefits of Collaborative Workflows

Collaborative workflows offer several advantages:

1. **Efficiency**: Combining the strengths of different Office applications can streamline processes and save time.

2. **Data Accuracy**: Integrating data from various sources helps ensure data consistency and accuracy.

3. **Enhanced Communication**: Collaborative workflows promote better communication and information sharing among team members.

4. **Customization**: Users can tailor workflows to their specific needs by leveraging the capabilities of different Office apps.

Integrating Data Across Applications

One of the fundamental aspects of collaborative workflows is integrating data across different Office applications. Here are some examples:

- **Linking Data**: You can link data from Excel spreadsheets into Word documents or PowerPoint presentations. This ensures that the data is always up-to-date, and changes made in Excel are reflected in the linked documents.

- **Access Data Integration**: If you use Microsoft Access to manage your data, you can integrate Access data into other Office apps. For instance, you can import Access data into Excel for analysis or create reports in Word using Access data.

Embedding Excel Data in Word and PowerPoint

Embedding Excel data in Word and PowerPoint is a common practice for creating dynamic documents and presentations. This allows you to maintain a live connection to the Excel data while presenting it in a more visually appealing format.

In Word, you can embed an Excel worksheet or chart as an object. This object remains linked to the original Excel file, and you can update it directly from Word.

In PowerPoint, you can insert Excel charts or tables into your slides. These objects can be linked to an Excel file, ensuring that your presentation always reflects the latest data.

Using Access Data in Excel and Word

Microsoft Access databases can store and manage large volumes of structured data. To leverage this data in other Office applications:

- **Excel**: You can import Access data into Excel to perform data analysis, create PivotTables, or generate reports. Excel's powerful functions and charts make it a valuable tool for working with Access data.

- **Word**: In Word, you can use Access data as a data source for mail merge operations. This is particularly useful for generating personalized letters, invoices, or labels based on Access data.

Dynamic Document Creation with Office

As discussed in Section 16.4, dynamic document creation is a powerful feature of Microsoft Office. Collaborative workflows often involve generating dynamic documents that incorporate data and content from various Office applications.

For example, you can create a report in Word that includes dynamic charts generated from Excel data, incorporates data from an Access database, and includes PowerPoint slides for visual explanations. Such integrated documents can be used for presentations, project reports, and business proposals.

Conclusion

Collaborative workflows that span across Microsoft Office applications enable teams to work together efficiently, leverage data from various sources, and create dynamic documents and presentations. By understanding how to integrate data, embed content, and utilize the strengths of each Office app, users can build powerful workflows tailored to their specific needs. This concludes our exploration of collaborative tools and techniques within the Microsoft Office ecosystem.

Chapter 17: Office on Different Platforms

Section 17.1: Using Office on Mac

Microsoft Office, a suite of productivity applications, is widely used across various platforms, including Windows and Mac. While the core functionalities of Office are consistent across platforms, there are some differences and unique features when using

Office on a Mac. In this section, we'll explore the usage of Microsoft Office on Mac computers.

Microsoft Office for Mac

Microsoft offers a dedicated version of Office for Mac users, known as Microsoft Office for Mac. This suite includes applications like Microsoft Word, Excel, PowerPoint, Outlook, and OneNote, tailored for macOS. Here are some key aspects to consider when using Office on a Mac:

1. User Interface: Office for Mac has a user interface that aligns with macOS design principles. It integrates with the Mac menu bar, toolbar, and provides a familiar experience for Mac users.

2. Cross-Platform Compatibility: Office for Mac ensures compatibility with documents created on Windows. You can seamlessly open, edit, and share documents with Windows users.

3. Cloud Integration: Just like the Windows version, Office for Mac supports cloud integration with OneDrive and SharePoint, enabling you to access your files from anywhere.

4. Collaboration: Office for Mac allows real-time collaboration on documents through co-authoring features in Word, Excel, and PowerPoint.

5. Touch Bar Support: On MacBooks with Touch Bar, Office apps offer Touch Bar shortcuts for quick access to commands and formatting options.

6. Dark Mode: Office for Mac takes advantage of macOS Dark Mode, providing a dark-themed interface for users who prefer it.

Microsoft 365 Subscription

To access the full range of features and benefits in Office for Mac, you'll need a Microsoft 365 subscription. Microsoft 365 provides additional services, including cloud storage, regular updates, and access to Office apps on multiple devices.

Installing Office on Mac

To install Office for Mac, follow these steps:

1. Purchase a Microsoft 365 subscription or check if you already have one.

2. Sign in to your Microsoft account associated with your subscription.

3. Go to the Microsoft 365 portal (https://portal.office.com).

4. Click on "Install Office" and select "Office for Mac."

5. Follow the on-screen instructions to download and install the Office applications.

Office for Mac takes advantage of macOS features, including Siri voice commands, Touch ID for document access, and iCloud integration for saving documents.

Conclusion

Using Microsoft Office on Mac is a seamless experience, with dedicated applications designed to work effectively within the macOS ecosystem. Whether you're creating documents, designing presentations, or managing emails, Office for Mac provides the tools you need for productivity on your Mac computer. In the following sections, we will explore Office applications on mobile devices and discuss cross-platform compatibility and limitations.

Section 17.2: Office Apps on Mobile Devices

In today's fast-paced world, mobile devices have become indispensable tools for productivity, communication, and collaboration. Microsoft Office recognizes the importance of mobile accessibility and offers a suite of Office apps designed for smartphones and tablets running iOS and Android. In this section, we'll explore Office apps on mobile devices and their capabilities.

Microsoft Office Mobile Apps

Microsoft provides mobile versions of its core Office applications, including Word, Excel, PowerPoint, and Outlook, as well as other productivity apps like OneNote and Teams. These apps are available for free on both iOS and Android devices, and they offer a range of features to help you stay productive while on the go.

1. Microsoft Word: The mobile version of Word allows you to create, edit, and format documents on your mobile device. It supports collaboration features, making it easy to work on documents with others in real-time.

2. Microsoft Excel: Excel on mobile devices lets you work with spreadsheets, perform calculations, and create charts. It's a powerful tool for data analysis on the go.

3. Microsoft PowerPoint: PowerPoint for mobile enables you to create and edit presentations, add slides, and incorporate multimedia elements. You can rehearse your presentation using Presenter Coach and present directly from your device.

4. Microsoft Outlook: Outlook on mobile provides email management, calendar functionality, and access to contacts and tasks. It syncs seamlessly with your desktop Outlook and web-based Office 365 account.

5. OneNote: OneNote is a versatile note-taking app available on mobile devices. You can create notebooks, jot down ideas, and access your notes across all your devices.

6. Microsoft Teams: Teams is Microsoft's collaboration platform, allowing you to chat, meet, and collaborate with your team on mobile devices. It's an essential tool for remote work and communication.

Here are some key features of Microsoft Office mobile apps:

- **Cloud Integration:** Office mobile apps integrate with OneDrive and SharePoint, allowing you to access and edit your documents stored in the cloud.

- **Touch-Optimized:** The apps are touch-optimized for mobile devices, making it easy to navigate and interact with documents using touch gestures.

- **Cross-Platform Compatibility:** Office mobile apps are compatible with documents created on Windows or macOS, ensuring seamless document sharing and collaboration.

- **Offline Access:** You can work on your documents offline, and changes will be synchronized once you're back online.

- **Security:** Microsoft prioritizes security, and Office mobile apps support features like biometric authentication and encryption to protect your data.

- **Productivity on the Go:** Whether you're on a business trip, in a meeting, or simply away from your desk, Office mobile apps empower you to be productive from anywhere.

To get started with Office mobile apps, follow these steps:

1. Go to your device's app store (App Store for iOS devices or Google Play Store for Android).

2. Search for the specific Office app you need, such as "Microsoft Word," "Microsoft Excel," or "Microsoft PowerPoint."

3. Download and install the app on your device.

4. Launch the app, sign in with your Microsoft account, and start using it.

Microsoft Office mobile apps bring the power of Office productivity to your smartphones and tablets. Whether you need to quickly review a document, make edits to a spreadsheet, or give a presentation on the go, these apps have you covered. They seamlessly integrate with other Office applications and the cloud, ensuring you can work efficiently and access your files wherever you are. In the next section, we'll explore cross-platform compatibility and limitations when using Office across different devices.

Section 17.3: Cross-Platform Compatibility and Limitations

As the way we work continues to evolve, the need for cross-platform compatibility in office productivity tools becomes increasingly important. Microsoft Office, the industry-standard suite of productivity applications, has made significant strides in ensuring that users can access and edit their documents seamlessly across different devices and platforms. In this section, we'll explore cross-platform compatibility in Microsoft Office and discuss some of the limitations you may encounter.

Cross-Platform Compatibility

Microsoft Office offers robust cross-platform compatibility, allowing users to access their documents on various devices and operating systems, including Windows, macOS, iOS, Android, and even on the web. Here's how it works:

1. Office for Windows and macOS: The desktop versions of Microsoft Office applications, such as Word, Excel, and PowerPoint, are available for both Windows and macOS. Documents created on one platform can be opened and edited on the other with full fidelity.

2. Office Online (Office for the Web): Microsoft provides a web-based version of Office called Office Online. It allows you to create, edit, and collaborate on documents directly in a web browser, regardless of your operating system. Office Online is compatible with major web browsers like Microsoft Edge, Google Chrome, Mozilla Firefox, and Apple Safari.

3. Office Mobile Apps: Microsoft offers mobile versions of its Office apps for iOS and Android devices. These apps are touch-optimized and provide a seamless experience for users on smartphones and tablets.

4. Cross-Platform Syncing: To ensure a consistent experience across devices, Microsoft offers cloud integration through OneDrive and SharePoint. This means that your documents are automatically synced between devices, ensuring you always have access to the latest version.

5. Real-Time Collaboration: One of the standout features of Microsoft Office is its real-time collaboration capabilities. Whether you're working on a document in Office Online, the desktop application, or a mobile app, you can collaborate with others in real time. This makes it easy for teams to work together, regardless of their device or location.

Limitations and Considerations

While Microsoft Office excels in cross-platform compatibility, there are some limitations and considerations to keep in mind:

1. Feature Parity: While Office Online and the mobile apps offer a wide range of features, they may not have the same extensive feature set as the desktop applications. Some advanced functionalities, especially in Excel and PowerPoint, may be limited in the online and mobile versions.

2. Offline Access: To take full advantage of cross-platform syncing and real-time collaboration, you need an internet connection. Offline access is available in some cases, but it may not offer the same level of functionality.

3. Formatting Compatibility: When moving between different platforms or using Office Online, you may encounter minor formatting differences in your documents. While Microsoft has made significant improvements in this area, it's essential to review your documents for any unexpected changes.

4. Integration with Third-Party Tools: Microsoft Office can integrate with a wide range of third-party tools and add-ins. However, the availability of these integrations may vary depending on the platform you're using.

5. Licensing and Subscription: To access the full suite of Office applications and features across different platforms, you may need a Microsoft 365 subscription. Licensing and subscription options can vary, so it's essential to choose the plan that suits your cross-platform needs.

Conclusion

Cross-platform compatibility is a crucial aspect of modern office productivity. Microsoft Office's commitment to ensuring that users can work seamlessly across Windows, macOS, iOS, Android, and the web is a significant advantage. By leveraging the desktop applications, Office Online, and mobile apps, you can access your documents from virtually anywhere, collaborate in real time, and stay productive regardless of your device. Understanding the limitations and considerations when working across platforms will help you make the most of this versatile suite of tools. In the next section, we'll explore the differences between cloud-based and desktop Office applications and their respective advantages.

Section 17.4: Cloud-Based Versus Desktop Office

The choice between cloud-based and desktop office applications is a decision many individuals and organizations face when adopting Microsoft Office. Each option comes with its own set of advantages and considerations. In this section, we'll explore the differences between these two approaches and help you make an informed choice based on your specific needs.

Desktop Office applications refer to the traditional software that you install on your computer, such as Microsoft Word, Excel, PowerPoint, and Outlook. Here are some key characteristics and considerations:

1. Offline Access: One of the primary advantages of desktop Office applications is their ability to work offline. Once installed, you don't need an internet connection to use these applications, making them suitable for scenarios where consistent internet access is not guaranteed.

2. Advanced Features: Desktop Office applications offer the most extensive feature sets. They are rich in functionalities and provide advanced capabilities for tasks like complex data analysis in Excel, detailed document formatting in Word, and sophisticated presentations in PowerPoint.

3. Customization: Desktop Office allows for extensive customization, including the creation of macros and custom add-ins using Visual Basic for Applications (VBA). This level of customization is often essential for organizations with specific workflow requirements.

4. Performance: Desktop applications typically offer better performance for resource-intensive tasks due to their direct integration with the local hardware.

5. Privacy and Security: With desktop applications, your data is stored locally, giving you more control over its security and privacy. Organizations with strict data handling requirements may prefer this approach.

6. Licensing: Desktop Office applications usually require a one-time purchase or subscription for access, and you can use them as long as you have a valid license. This licensing model can be cost-effective over time.

Cloud-based Office applications, on the other hand, refer to tools like Office Online (web-based apps) and Office 365 (now known as Microsoft 365), which are accessed via a web browser. Here's what you need to know about them:

1. Cross-Platform Access: Cloud-based Office applications are accessible from any device with an internet connection and a web browser. This makes them highly versatile and suitable for users who need to work on various platforms.

2. Real-Time Collaboration: One of the standout features of cloud-based Office is real-time collaboration. Multiple users can work on the same document simultaneously, facilitating teamwork and remote collaboration.

3. Automatic Updates: Cloud-based applications are updated automatically by Microsoft, ensuring that users always have access to the latest features and security patches without manual installations.

4. Document Synchronization: Cloud-based Office applications integrate seamlessly with OneDrive, SharePoint, and other cloud storage solutions, allowing for easy document synchronization across devices.

5. Subscription Model: Many cloud-based Office offerings, such as Microsoft 365, operate on a subscription model. Users pay a recurring fee for access, which can be advantageous for staying up to date but may lead to higher long-term costs.

6. Limited Offline Access: While some cloud-based applications offer limited offline functionality, they are primarily designed for online use. This can be a drawback in areas with unreliable internet connectivity.

Making the Choice

The choice between desktop and cloud-based Office applications depends on your specific needs and preferences. Here are some factors to consider when making your decision:

1. Connectivity: Consider the reliability of your internet connection. If you frequently work offline or in areas with poor connectivity, desktop applications may be more suitable.

2. Collaboration: If you collaborate extensively with others, especially remotely, cloud-based Office applications offer superior real-time collaboration features.

3. Customization: Evaluate whether you require advanced customization options provided by desktop applications, such as VBA scripting.

4. Licensing Costs: Compare the licensing costs of desktop applications with the subscription fees associated with cloud-based options to determine which is more cost-effective for your organization.

5. Platform Diversity: If you work on various devices and operating systems, cloud-based Office may provide a more consistent experience.

6. Security and Privacy: Consider your organization's data security and privacy requirements. Some industries and organizations may prefer the control offered by desktop applications.

In conclusion, both desktop and cloud-based Office applications have their strengths and limitations. The choice ultimately depends on your specific workflow, connectivity, collaboration needs, and budget considerations. Understanding these differences will help you select the right approach to harness the full potential of Microsoft Office for your productivity needs.

Section 17.5: Accessibility Features in Office

Microsoft Office has made significant strides in enhancing its accessibility features to ensure that individuals with disabilities can fully utilize its suite of applications. Accessibility is a crucial aspect of modern software design, and Microsoft has integrated a variety of tools and features to support users with diverse needs. In this section, we'll explore the accessibility features available in Microsoft Office.

Accessibility Checker

One of the key accessibility tools in Office applications is the **Accessibility Checker**. It's designed to help you identify and fix accessibility issues in your documents, spreadsheets, presentations, and emails. Here's how it works:

1. **Accessibility Recommendations:** When you run the Accessibility Checker, it provides a list of recommendations to improve the accessibility of your content. These recommendations include adding alternative text to images, ensuring proper heading structure, and using meaningful hyperlink text.

2. **Step-by-Step Guidance:** The tool offers step-by-step guidance on how to fix each issue it identifies. It helps you understand why a particular change is necessary and how to implement it.

3. **Document Scanning:** The Accessibility Checker scans your entire document or presentation and highlights any potential problems. It provides a clear overview of issues that need attention.

Accessibility Features by Application

Each Office application offers specific accessibility features:

1. Microsoft Word:
- **Read Aloud:** Word includes a Read Aloud feature that reads your document out loud, making it accessible to individuals with visual impairments or learning disabilities.
- **Navigation Features:** Word provides keyboard shortcuts and navigation features for screen reader users, enabling efficient document navigation.

2. Microsoft Excel:
- **Screen Reader Support:** Excel is compatible with screen readers like JAWS and NVDA, ensuring that users can navigate and interact with spreadsheets using assistive technology.
- **Accessible Charts:** You can create accessible charts with descriptive titles, data labels, and alternative text for data points.

3. Microsoft PowerPoint:
- **Slide Layouts:** PowerPoint offers predefined slide layouts that are designed for accessibility. Using these layouts ensures proper reading order and structure.

- **Alt Text for Multimedia:** You can add alternative text to images, videos, and audio in your presentations, making them accessible to all.

4. *Microsoft Outlook:*

- **Keyboard Shortcuts:** Outlook provides keyboard shortcuts for common actions, enhancing accessibility for users who rely on keyboard navigation.
- **Screen Reader Support:** Like other Office applications, Outlook works well with screen readers, enabling users to manage emails, calendars, and contacts effectively.

Accessibility Resources

Microsoft offers extensive resources for users and developers to enhance accessibility:

- **Accessibility Training:** Microsoft provides free training resources and tutorials on creating accessible content in Office applications.
- **Accessibility User Guide:** The Office Accessibility Center offers comprehensive guides for users with disabilities, including step-by-step instructions and best practices.
- **Developer Resources:** Developers can access the Accessibility Developer Hub, which provides guidance on building accessible Office add-ins and solutions.

Conclusion

Microsoft Office's commitment to accessibility ensures that everyone, regardless of their abilities, can use its applications effectively. By utilizing the built-in accessibility tools and following best practices, you can create content that is inclusive and meets the needs of a diverse audience. Whether you're a content creator or an end user, taking advantage of these features contributes to a more accessible and inclusive digital environment.

Chapter 18: Customizing and Extending Office 365

Section 18.1: Exploring Office 365 Administration

Office 365, now known as Microsoft 365, is a powerful suite of cloud-based productivity tools that offers a wide range of features and capabilities to individuals and organizations. Managing an Office 365 environment effectively requires a solid understanding of its administration tools and settings. In this section, we will delve into Office 365 administration and explore key concepts, tools, and best practices for managing your Office 365 subscription.

Office 365 Admin Center

The central hub for managing Office 365 is the **Office 365 Admin Center**. This web-based portal provides administrators with a comprehensive set of tools to configure, monitor, and maintain their Office 365 services. Here are some essential features of the Admin Center:

1. **Dashboard:** The dashboard provides an overview of your organization's Office 365 status, including active users, service health, and recent service incidents.

2. **Users and Groups:** You can manage user accounts, assign licenses, and create and manage security groups and distribution lists.

3. **Settings:** Configure settings for various Office 365 services, including Exchange Online, SharePoint Online, and Microsoft Teams.

4. **Reports:** Access reports and analytics to gain insights into user activity, email usage, and more. Reports help you monitor the health and performance of your Office 365 environment.

5. **Security & Compliance:** Implement security measures such as multi-factor authentication, data loss prevention, and threat protection to safeguard your organization's data.

License Management

One of the critical tasks in Office 365 administration is managing licenses. Licenses determine which Office 365 services and applications users can access. Here's how license management works:

- **Assigning Licenses:** You can assign licenses to individual users or assign licenses based on groups or roles within your organization.

- **License Types:** Office 365 offers various license types, such as E3, E5, Business Premium, and more, each with its set of features and applications.

- **Monitoring License Usage:** The Admin Center allows you to monitor license usage to ensure that you are not over-allocating licenses.

User Management

User management is another important aspect of Office 365 administration. You can:

- **Create and Delete Users:** Add new users to your Office 365 subscription and remove accounts for employees who have left your organization.

- **User Roles:** Assign administrative roles to users based on their responsibilities, granting them specific permissions to manage Office 365 services.

- **Password Policies:** Implement password policies and security features to protect user accounts.

Data Migration

If you are migrating from an on-premises environment to Office 365 or between Office 365 tenants, data migration becomes a crucial task. Microsoft offers various tools and methods to facilitate data migration, including:

- **Exchange Online Migration:** Migrate email data from on-premises Exchange servers to Exchange Online.

- **SharePoint and OneDrive Migration:** Move documents and files from on-premises SharePoint servers or file shares to SharePoint Online and OneDrive for Business.

- **Third-Party Migration Tools:** Many third-party tools are available to simplify and automate data migration tasks.

Collaboration and Communication Settings

Office 365 includes collaboration and communication tools like Microsoft Teams, SharePoint Online, and Yammer. Administrators can configure settings, permissions, and policies to govern how these tools are used within the organization. Collaboration settings often include:

- **Microsoft Teams:** Customize Teams settings, create channels, and control guest access.

- **SharePoint Online:** Configure site collections, libraries, and document sharing settings.

- **Yammer:** Manage communities, user access, and integration with other Office 365 services.

Compliance and Data Governance

Compliance and data governance are essential for organizations to meet regulatory requirements and maintain data security. Office 365 offers tools for compliance management, including:

- **Data Loss Prevention (DLP):** Create DLP policies to prevent the sharing of sensitive information.

- **eDiscovery:** Conduct electronic discovery searches to find and preserve data for legal and compliance purposes.

- **Retention Policies:** Define retention policies to control data lifecycle and automatic deletion.

Support and Service Health

Lastly, the Admin Center provides access to support resources and service health information. Administrators can:

- **Contact Support:** Open service requests with Microsoft Support for assistance with issues or technical challenges.

- **Service Health Dashboard:** Monitor the status of Office 365 services and receive notifications of incidents or outages affecting your organization.

In this section, we've introduced the Office 365 Admin Center and highlighted key aspects of Office 365 administration, including license management, user management, data migration, collaboration settings, compliance, and support. As organizations increasingly rely on cloud-based productivity tools, effective administration of Office 365 becomes vital for optimizing the user experience, ensuring data security, and achieving business goals.

Section 18.2: Customizing User Experience in Office 365

Customizing the user experience in Office 365 allows organizations to tailor the platform to their specific needs and branding, enhancing productivity and user satisfaction. In this section, we will explore various ways to customize the user experience in Office 365, from adjusting the appearance and functionality to incorporating custom branding and features.

Office 365 App Customization

1. **App Launcher:** The Office 365 App Launcher is a customizable menu that provides quick access to apps. Administrators can add, remove, or rearrange app icons to ensure that users have easy access to the tools they need most.

2. **App Settings:** For each individual app, there are settings that allow administrators to configure the default behavior and appearance. This includes options like enabling or disabling features, adjusting security settings, and controlling user access.

Custom Branding

3. **Branding Policies:** Organizations can create branding policies to apply custom themes, logos, and colors to Office 365 applications, giving them a personalized look and feel.

4. **Custom Sign-In Page:** Customize the Office 365 sign-in page with your organization's branding, creating a seamless user experience that aligns with your corporate identity.

User Permissions and Settings

5. **User Permissions:** Administrators can fine-tune user permissions to control who can access specific features or perform certain actions within Office 365 applications. This helps maintain security and privacy.

6. **User Settings:** Users can personalize their Office 365 experience by adjusting settings such as language preferences, time zones, and notification preferences.

SharePoint Online Customization

7. **Site Templates:** Customize SharePoint Online sites by creating custom site templates with predefined layouts, libraries, and settings. This simplifies the process of creating consistent sites across your organization.

8. **Site Designs:** Use site designs to apply custom branding, add lists and libraries, or create new pages when a user creates a new site. This ensures that every site adheres to your organization's standards.

Power Platform Customization

9. **Power Apps:** Build custom apps using Power Apps to streamline business processes and integrate them into Office 365. These apps can be tailored to your organization's unique needs.

10. **Power Automate:** Automate workflows and tasks within Office 365 using Power Automate. Create custom flows that connect Office 365 applications and external services to improve efficiency.

Custom Development

11. **Microsoft Graph API:** For advanced customization and integration, developers can leverage the Microsoft Graph API to access and manipulate Office 365 data programmatically. This allows for the creation of custom applications and solutions.

12. **Office Add-Ins:** Extend the functionality of Office applications by developing custom add-ins. These add-ins can provide additional features and integrations within Word, Excel, Outlook, and other Office programs.

Training and Adoption

13. **Training Resources:** To ensure a successful rollout of customizations, provide training and documentation to users. Help them understand how to make the most of the tailored Office 365 experience.

14. **User Feedback:** Encourage users to provide feedback on the customizations. Their input can help identify areas for improvement and refinements in the user experience.

Continuous Improvement

15. **Monitoring and Analytics:** Regularly monitor the usage and performance of customizations. Use analytics to assess their impact on productivity and identify areas where further customization or optimization may be needed.

16. **Feedback Loop:** Maintain an ongoing feedback loop with users and administrators to gather insights and suggestions for enhancing the customized Office 365 experience.

Customizing the user experience in Office 365 is an ongoing process that requires a balance between meeting organizational needs and providing users with a familiar and efficient environment. By utilizing the various customization options available and continuously refining them based on feedback and analytics, organizations can optimize their Office 365 deployment to boost productivity and user satisfaction.

Section 18.3: Security and Compliance in the Cloud

Ensuring security and compliance in the cloud is a top priority for organizations using Office 365. Microsoft provides a range of tools and features to help organizations protect their data, meet regulatory requirements, and maintain a secure environment. In this section, we will delve into the key aspects of security and compliance within Office 365.

Data Protection and Encryption

1. **Data Loss Prevention (DLP):** Office 365 offers DLP policies that allow organizations to define and enforce rules for protecting sensitive information. DLP policies can automatically block or restrict the sharing of confidential data, ensuring it doesn't leave the organization.

2. **Encryption:** Data at rest and in transit is encrypted in Office 365. This includes email messages, files stored in OneDrive and SharePoint, and data transmitted between Microsoft's data centers and client devices.

Identity and Access Management

3. **Multi-Factor Authentication (MFA):** Implementing MFA adds an extra layer of security by requiring users to provide multiple forms of verification before gaining access to their Office 365 accounts. This helps protect against unauthorized access due to compromised passwords.

4. **Conditional Access:** With Conditional Access policies, organizations can control access to Office 365 based on various conditions, such as device compliance, location, and user roles. This enhances security while ensuring a seamless user experience.

Threat Protection

5. **Exchange Online Protection (EOP):** EOP is a built-in security feature for Exchange Online that helps safeguard email communication by blocking malware, phishing attempts, and spam.

6. **Advanced Threat Protection (ATP):** ATP extends email protection with features like safe attachments and safe links, which protect against malicious attachments and links in emails.

7. **Threat Intelligence:** Office 365 Threat Intelligence provides insights into global threat trends and helps organizations proactively defend against cyber threats.

Compliance and Data Governance

8. **eDiscovery:** Office 365 includes eDiscovery tools that enable organizations to search, hold, and export data for legal and compliance purposes. This is crucial for meeting regulatory requirements.

9. **Retention and Archiving:** Define retention policies to automatically retain or delete content based on business or regulatory requirements. Archiving ensures that historical data is preserved and easily accessible.

10. **Audit Logs:** Office 365 captures detailed audit logs of user and admin activities. These logs can be used for security investigations, compliance reporting, and monitoring user behavior.

11. **Security and Compliance Center:** The Security and Compliance Center in Office 365 provides a centralized hub for managing security and compliance settings, policies, and reports.

User Training and Awareness

12. **Security Awareness Training:** Educate users about best practices for security, such as recognizing phishing attempts and reporting suspicious activities. Well-informed users are a critical line of defense.

Third-Party Integration

13. **Third-Party Security Solutions:** Organizations can integrate third-party security solutions with Office 365 to enhance protection further. These solutions can provide additional layers of security and compliance capabilities.

Continuous Monitoring and Improvement

14. **Security Baseline Assessments:** Regularly assess the security configuration of Office 365 to identify and address vulnerabilities. Microsoft provides security baseline recommendations to help organizations improve their security posture.

15. **Incident Response Plan:** Develop a comprehensive incident response plan to quickly and effectively respond to security incidents, minimizing potential damage.

Security and compliance in Office 365 are ongoing responsibilities. Organizations must regularly review and update their security policies, educate users, and stay informed about emerging threats. By leveraging the built-in security features and best practices, organizations can maintain a secure and compliant environment in the cloud while harnessing the full capabilities of Office 365.

Section 18.4: Extending Office 365 with Third-Party Apps

While Office 365 provides a wide range of features and tools to meet the needs of most organizations, there are cases where specific requirements or niche functionalities can be addressed by third-party applications and integrations. In this section, we'll explore the concept of extending Office 365 with third-party apps and how it can enhance productivity and functionality.

1. **Specialized Functionality:** Third-party apps can offer specialized features and capabilities that cater to unique business needs. These apps are often developed by experts in a particular domain, providing deep functionality.

2. **Integration Options:** Many third-party apps are designed to seamlessly integrate with Office 365, enhancing the overall user experience. Integration can involve single sign-on, data sharing, and workflow automation.

3. **Enhanced Productivity:** By leveraging third-party apps, organizations can streamline processes, automate repetitive tasks, and improve overall productivity. These apps can address specific pain points and reduce manual effort.

4. **Scalability:** Third-party app developers often provide updates and enhancements, ensuring that the solution remains relevant and can scale as your organization grows.

Common Use Cases

1. Customer Relationship Management (CRM)

CRM systems like Salesforce, HubSpot, and Dynamics 365 can be integrated with Office 365 to centralize customer data, streamline sales processes, and enhance customer interactions. This integration ensures that sales, marketing, and support teams have access to up-to-date customer information directly within their Office 365 environment.

2. Project Management

Tools like Asana, Trello, or Jira can complement Office 365 by providing robust project management and collaboration features. Integration allows project teams to work efficiently, track tasks, and share project updates seamlessly.

3. Document Management

Document management systems such as SharePoint, Box, or Dropbox can enhance document collaboration, version control, and access control within Office 365. These integrations ensure that documents are stored and organized effectively.

4. Email Marketing

Third-party email marketing platforms like MailChimp or Constant Contact can be integrated with Office 365 to manage email campaigns, track engagement, and analyze the effectiveness of marketing efforts. This integration simplifies the process of reaching and engaging with customers.

5. Analytics and Reporting

Analytics tools like Power BI can be used in conjunction with Office 365 to create interactive reports and dashboards. This empowers organizations to make data-driven decisions and gain insights from their Office 365 data.

When evaluating and implementing third-party apps within your Office 365 environment, consider the following:

1. **Security and Compliance:** Ensure that third-party apps adhere to your organization's security and compliance requirements. Verify their data handling practices, access controls, and encryption methods.

2. **Integration Compatibility:** Confirm that the third-party app integrates smoothly with your Office 365 setup. Evaluate the available connectors, APIs, and compatibility with your existing infrastructure.

3. **User Training:** Provide adequate training and resources to users who will be utilizing these third-party apps. User adoption is crucial for realizing the benefits of these integrations.

4. **Cost and Licensing:** Understand the pricing structure of third-party apps, including any licensing fees or subscription costs. Consider the return on investment (ROI) in terms of productivity gains and improved functionality.

5. **Support and Maintenance:** Assess the availability of support and maintenance from the third-party app provider. This includes updates, patches, and troubleshooting assistance.

By carefully selecting and integrating third-party apps that align with your organization's goals and needs, you can extend the capabilities of Office 365 and create a more tailored and efficient digital workplace. These integrations can contribute to improved collaboration, productivity, and competitiveness in the modern business landscape.

Section 18.5: Migrating to Office 365: Best Practices

Migrating to Office 365 is a significant undertaking for organizations of all sizes. Whether you are transitioning from an on-premises environment or from another cloud-based solution, proper planning and execution are essential to ensure a smooth migration process. In this section, we will explore best practices for migrating to Office 365.

1. Assessment and Planning

Before you begin the migration process, it's crucial to assess your current environment and plan accordingly:

*   **Inventory Assessment:** Conduct a thorough inventory of your existing infrastructure, including servers, applications, and data repositories. Identify what needs to be migrated and what can be retired or replaced.

- **User Needs Analysis:** Understand the requirements and expectations of your users. Identify any specialized applications or workflows that may require special attention during migration.

- **Licensing and Subscription Planning:** Determine the appropriate Office 365 subscription and licensing model for your organization based on user needs and compliance requirements.

2. Data Migration Strategy

The heart of any Office 365 migration is the data. Here are key considerations for a successful data migration:

- **Data Cleanup:** Before migrating data, clean up and organize it. Remove redundant, outdated, and trivial (ROT) data. This reduces the volume of data to be migrated and streamlines the process.

- **Data Categorization:** Categorize your data into different groups based on importance and access requirements. This helps prioritize migration efforts and access control.

- **Migration Tools:** Consider using migration tools provided by Microsoft or third-party vendors. These tools can automate data migration, ensure data fidelity, and minimize downtime.

3. Email Migration

Email migration is often a core part of Office 365 migration. Here are some specific considerations:

- **Migration Methods:** Depending on your existing email system (e.g., Exchange, IMAP, or other platforms), choose the appropriate migration method: cutover, staged, hybrid, or IMAP migration.

- **Testing:** Before migrating all email accounts, perform pilot migrations to validate the process, ensure email fidelity, and identify and resolve any issues.

- **DNS Changes:** Be prepared to update DNS records to direct email traffic to Office 365 once the migration is complete.

4. User Training and Communication

A successful migration includes preparing and informing your users:

- **Training:** Provide training and resources to help users transition to Office 365 smoothly. This includes guidance on using Office applications, email, and collaboration tools.

- **Communication:** Communicate the migration plan, timelines, and expected changes to users well in advance. Address common concerns and provide support channels for questions and issues.

5. Security and Compliance

Ensure that security and compliance requirements are met throughout the migration process:

- **Data Protection:** Implement data loss prevention (DLP) policies to safeguard sensitive information during migration and after it's in Office 365.

- **Compliance Auditing:** Continuously monitor and audit Office 365 to ensure compliance with industry regulations and organizational policies.

6. Testing and Validation

Testing is critical to identify and resolve issues before they impact users:

- **Testing Environments:** Set up test environments that mimic the production environment for thorough testing of applications and services.

- **User Acceptance Testing (UAT):** Involve end-users in UAT to ensure that applications and workflows function as expected.

7. Rollout and Monitoring

Once you are ready to migrate, follow these steps:

- **Phased Rollout:** Consider a phased migration approach, starting with a pilot group of users and gradually expanding to the entire organization.

- **Monitoring:** Continuously monitor the Office 365 environment for performance, security, and compliance. Use monitoring tools and services to proactively identify and resolve issues.

8. Post-Migration Support

After migration, ongoing support and optimization are key:

- **User Support:** Offer post-migration support to address user questions and issues promptly.

- **Optimization:** Regularly review and optimize your Office 365 configuration to align with changing business needs and evolving Office 365 features.

By following these best practices, organizations can ensure a successful and efficient migration to Office 365. A well-executed migration can lead to increased productivity, collaboration, and agility, allowing businesses to fully leverage the benefits of the Office 365 ecosystem.

Chapter 19: Troubleshooting and Support

Section 19.1: Common Issues in Office Applications

Office applications are powerful tools, but like any software, they can encounter issues and errors. Understanding common problems and how to troubleshoot them is essential for maintaining productivity. In this section, we will explore some of the most frequent issues users face with Office applications and provide guidance on how to address them.

1. Application Crashes

Problem: Office applications, such as Word or Excel, occasionally crash or become unresponsive.

Solution:

- **Check for Updates:** Ensure that your Office application is up to date. Microsoft often releases updates that address stability issues.
- **Add-ins:** Disable any recently installed add-ins or extensions, as they can sometimes conflict with Office. Re-enable them one by one to identify the problematic one.
- **Repair Office:** You can use the built-in repair feature to fix corrupted Office installations. Go to "Control Panel" (Windows) or "Applications" (Mac), find Microsoft Office, and select the repair option.
- **Hardware Acceleration:** Disable hardware acceleration in Office settings, as it might be causing conflicts with certain graphics drivers.

2. Document Corruption

Problem: Documents may become corrupted, leading to errors when trying to open or edit them.

Solution:

- **AutoRecover:** Office applications have an AutoRecover feature that can help recover unsaved changes in case of a crash. Look for the recovered files in the respective application's recovery folder.
- **Backup Copies:** Regularly back up your important documents to prevent data loss due to corruption. Services like OneDrive or SharePoint can automate this process.
- **File Format:** Use standard and widely supported file formats like .docx (Word) or .xlsx (Excel) to reduce the risk of corruption.

3. Performance Issues

Problem: Office applications may become slow or sluggish, affecting productivity.

Solution:

- **Hardware Requirements:** Ensure that your computer meets the minimum hardware requirements for running Office efficiently. Upgrading hardware, such as RAM or SSD, can significantly improve performance.
- **Add-ins:** Disable unnecessary add-ins or extensions that might be consuming system resources. Some add-ins run automatically and can slow down Office.
- **Large Files:** If you're working with large files, consider optimizing them. For example, compress images in a PowerPoint presentation or use Excel's data optimization tools.
- **Clean Cache:** Clear temporary files and cache regularly. Office applications accumulate temporary data that can impact performance over time.

4. Compatibility Issues

Problem: Compatibility problems can occur when sharing Office documents with others who use different versions or software.

Solution:

- **Save in Compatibility Mode:** When saving documents, use the "Compatibility Mode" or "Save As" options to choose older file formats that are compatible with earlier Office versions.
- **PDF Conversion:** If compatibility is a concern, consider saving documents as PDF files, which have consistent formatting across different platforms.
- **Online Collaboration:** Use Office 365 or Office Online for collaborative work. These online platforms ensure that all users are working with the same, up-to-date version of the document.

5. Activation and Licensing

Problem: Issues related to product activation or licensing can prevent you from using Office applications.

Solution:

- **Check License Status:** Ensure that your Office subscription is active and that you are signed in with the correct Microsoft account associated with the subscription.
- **Reactivation:** If you've recently made hardware changes to your computer, you may need to reactivate Office. Follow the prompts to reactivate online or by phone.

6. Printer and Page Layout Problems

Problem: Printing from Office applications or issues with page layout can be frustrating.

Solution:

- **Printer Drivers:** Ensure that you have the latest printer drivers installed for your device. Outdated drivers can cause printing problems.
- **Print Preview:** Use the Print Preview feature to check how your document will appear before printing. Adjust margins and settings as needed.

- **Page Breaks:** Use manual page breaks or section breaks to control page layout, especially in complex documents.

7. Network and Connectivity Issues

Problem: Office applications may have trouble connecting to online services, such as OneDrive or SharePoint.

Solution:

- **Internet Connection:** Verify that you have a stable internet connection. Poor connectivity can lead to synchronization issues.
- **Firewalls and Antivirus:** Ensure that your firewall or antivirus software is not blocking Office from accessing the internet. Add exceptions if necessary.
- **Office Updates:** Keep Office applications up to date, as updates often include improvements in connectivity and online services.

By familiarizing yourself with these common issues and their solutions, you can troubleshoot and resolve problems efficiently, minimizing downtime and frustration when working with Office applications. If a particular issue persists, don't hesitate to seek assistance from Microsoft support or your organization's IT department.

Section 19.2: Effective Troubleshooting Techniques

When faced with issues in Microsoft Office applications, it's essential to have effective troubleshooting techniques at your disposal. Troubleshooting can be a systematic process that helps identify and resolve problems efficiently. In this section, we will discuss various troubleshooting methods that can be applied to common Office application issues.

1. Identify the Problem

The first step in troubleshooting is to identify the specific problem you are experiencing. Is it an error message, a crash, or unexpected behavior? Take note of any error codes or messages as they can provide valuable information.

2. Check for Updates

Ensure that your Office applications are up to date. Microsoft regularly releases updates to address bugs and improve stability. To check for updates:

- For Windows: Open any Office application, go to "File" > "Account," and click on "Update Options." Choose "Update Now" to check for updates.
- For Mac: Open the Microsoft AutoUpdate application to check for updates.

3. Restart the Application

Sometimes, simply closing and reopening the problematic Office application can resolve minor issues. Close all open documents, exit the application, and then relaunch it.

4. Restart Your Computer

If restarting the application doesn't work, try restarting your computer. This can clear temporary issues in the system that might be affecting Office.

5. Check for Conflicting Add-ins

Add-ins or extensions can sometimes conflict with Office applications and cause problems. Disable third-party add-ins and restart the application to see if the issue is resolved. You can manage add-ins through the application's settings or preferences.

6. Use Safe Mode (Windows)

In Windows, you can start Office applications in Safe Mode to troubleshoot issues caused by add-ins or customization. To do this, press the Windows key, type the name of the Office application (e.g., "Word"), and add "/safe" after it (e.g., "winword.exe /safe"). This will start the application without loading any add-ins.

7. Repair Office Installation

If the issue persists, you can repair the Office installation. This can help fix corrupted files or settings. To repair Office:

- For Windows: Open the "Control Panel," find "Programs and Features" (or "Add or Remove Programs"), locate Microsoft Office, right-click, and select "Change." Choose the repair option.
- For Mac: Open "Applications," find Microsoft Office, and run the "Microsoft Office Setup Assistant." Choose the repair option.

8. Check for Compatibility

If you are working with files created in a different version of Office, ensure that compatibility settings are correctly configured. Use the "Compatibility Mode" or "Save As" options to save files in older formats if needed.

9. Use Online Repair (Windows)

In Windows, you can perform an online repair of Office if the built-in repair option doesn't work. To do this, go to "Control Panel," find "Programs and Features," locate Microsoft Office, right-click, and select "Change." Choose the online repair option.

10. Check for System Updates

Ensure that your operating system is also up to date. System updates can provide fixes for issues related to compatibility and security.

11. Check for Hardware Issues

Sometimes, hardware problems, such as a failing hard drive or faulty RAM, can manifest as software issues. Run hardware diagnostics to rule out any hardware-related problems.

12. Seek Online Resources

If you are still unable to resolve the problem, consider searching online for solutions. Microsoft's official support website and user forums often provide step-by-step guides for troubleshooting specific issues.

13. Contact Support

If all else fails, don't hesitate to contact Microsoft support or your organization's IT department for assistance. Provide them with detailed information about the problem and any error messages you've encountered.

14. Backup Your Data

Before attempting major troubleshooting steps or repairs, ensure that you have a backup of your important Office documents to prevent data loss.

Effective troubleshooting is a valuable skill when working with Microsoft Office applications. By following a systematic approach and using the techniques mentioned above, you can quickly diagnose and resolve problems, minimizing disruptions to your work.

Section 19.3: Seeking Help: Resources and Communities

When you encounter challenging issues with Microsoft Office applications, seeking help from various resources and communities can be invaluable. This section explores the different avenues available for obtaining assistance and solutions to your Office-related problems.

1. Official Microsoft Support

Microsoft offers official support for its products, including Office. Visit the Microsoft Support website, where you can search for solutions to common issues, access troubleshooting guides, and use the virtual assistant for personalized assistance.

2. Microsoft Community

The Microsoft Community is a user-driven forum where individuals can ask questions and seek help from the Office community. You can browse existing discussions or post your own questions to get responses from experienced users and Microsoft MVPs (Most Valuable Professionals).

3. Office Help Center

The Office Help Center provides detailed guides, tutorials, and articles on various Office applications and topics. You can find step-by-step instructions for troubleshooting specific issues and optimizing your Office experience.

4. Online Forums

Apart from Microsoft's official community, several online forums are dedicated to Office-related discussions. Websites like TechNet, Spiceworks, and Experts Exchange host active communities where IT professionals and users share their knowledge and offer assistance.

5. Social Media

Platforms like Twitter, Reddit, and LinkedIn have active Office-related communities and groups. You can search for relevant hashtags or join Office-related groups to connect with experts and enthusiasts.

6. YouTube Tutorials

YouTube hosts numerous Office-related tutorial channels where experts demonstrate solutions to common problems and provide tips and tricks. Video tutorials can be especially helpful for visual learners.

7. Online Courses

Consider enrolling in online courses or training programs dedicated to Microsoft Office. Platforms like LinkedIn Learning, Udemy, and Coursera offer a wide range of Office courses, including troubleshooting and advanced usage.

8. Local User Groups

Check if there are local Microsoft Office user groups or meetups in your area. Joining these groups can provide opportunities for in-person networking and knowledge sharing.

9. Consult Your Organization's IT Support

If you are using Office in a corporate environment, your organization likely has an IT support team. Don't hesitate to reach out to them for assistance, especially if the issue is affecting multiple users.

10. Third-Party Support Services

In some cases, you might need to seek assistance from third-party IT support services or consultants who specialize in Microsoft Office. They can provide customized solutions for complex issues.

11. Check Online Documentation

Many Office add-ins and plugins have online documentation and knowledge bases. If you are encountering problems with specific add-ons, visit their respective websites for troubleshooting guides and FAQs.

12. Review Error Messages

When encountering errors, take note of any error messages or codes. You can often find specific solutions by searching for the error message online or on Microsoft's official support site.

13. Stay Informed

Keep yourself updated about the latest Office developments, updates, and best practices. This knowledge can help you avoid common issues and make the most of new features.

Remember that troubleshooting often requires patience and persistence. When seeking help from communities and forums, be sure to provide clear and detailed information about your issue, including the Office application version, operating system, and any error messages received. This will increase the likelihood of receiving relevant and helpful responses.

Utilizing these resources and communities effectively can enhance your Office troubleshooting skills and ensure that you can resolve issues promptly, allowing you to stay productive and make the most of Microsoft Office's capabilities.

Section 19.4: Upgrading and Updating Office Applications

Regularly updating and upgrading your Microsoft Office applications is essential to ensure you have access to the latest features, security patches, and bug fixes. This section covers the importance of keeping your Office software up to date and provides guidance on how to perform updates and upgrades.

1. Why Updates and Upgrades Matter

Microsoft regularly releases updates and upgrades for Office applications to enhance functionality and security. These updates address known vulnerabilities, improve performance, and introduce new features or improvements. Staying up to date is crucial for the following reasons:

- **Security**: Updates often include security patches that protect your system from threats and vulnerabilities. Ignoring updates can leave your computer at risk.

- **Bug Fixes**: Updates fix software bugs and glitches that may affect your productivity or the accuracy of your work.

- **New Features**: Upgrades introduce new features, tools, and capabilities that can streamline your workflow and improve your overall experience.

2. How to Update Office

Keeping your Office applications updated is relatively straightforward:

- **Automatic Updates**: By default, Office applications are set to receive automatic updates from Microsoft. These updates are installed silently in the background, ensuring you have the latest version without manual intervention.

- **Manual Updates**: If you want to check for updates manually, open any Office application (e.g., Word or Excel), go to the "File" tab, select "Account" (or "Office Account" in some versions), and click on the "Update Options" button. Choose "Update Now" to check for and install available updates.

- **Office Update Tool**: Microsoft provides the "Office Update Tool," which allows you to manually download and install updates for Office. You can find this tool on the Microsoft Office support website.

- **Office 365 Subscription**: If you have an Office 365 subscription, you receive the latest updates as part of your subscription. Ensure that your subscription is active to continue receiving updates.

3. How to Upgrade Office

Upgrading Office typically involves moving to a newer version or edition of the software. Here's how you can upgrade Office:

- **Purchase a Newer Version**: When Microsoft releases a new version of Office (e.g., upgrading from Office 2019 to Office 2021), you can purchase the new version directly from Microsoft's website or an authorized retailer. Follow the installation instructions provided with your purchase.

- **Office 365**: If you are using Office 365, you are entitled to receive the latest versions of Office as long as your subscription is active. Your Office applications will be automatically updated to the most recent version.

- **Volume Licensing**: In enterprise environments, upgrading Office may involve volume licensing agreements. Organizations can work with Microsoft representatives to plan and execute Office upgrades for multiple users.

4. Best Practices for Updates and Upgrades

To ensure a smooth transition during updates and upgrades, consider these best practices:

- **Backup Your Data**: Before performing any major update or upgrade, create backups of your important documents and data to prevent data loss.

- **Check System Requirements**: Ensure that your computer meets the system requirements for the new version of Office before upgrading.

- **Plan for Downtime**: For organizations, schedule updates and upgrades during periods of low usage to minimize disruptions.

- **Test in Advance**: In business settings, test the new version of Office with a small group of users to identify and resolve any compatibility issues before deploying it to the entire organization.

- **Stay Informed**: Keep track of Microsoft's official announcements and release notes to understand the changes and improvements introduced in new Office versions.

By following these guidelines, you can keep your Office applications up to date and smoothly transition to newer versions when necessary, ensuring that you benefit from the latest features and maintain a secure and productive computing environment.

Section 19.5: Office Application Recovery and Data Loss Prevention

Accidents happen, and data loss can occur even in well-maintained computer systems. This section focuses on strategies and tools for recovering lost Office documents and preventing data loss. Whether you accidentally deleted a crucial document or encountered a system failure, knowing how to recover your work is invaluable.

1. AutoRecover and Document Recovery

Office applications, such as Microsoft Word and Excel, offer an AutoRecover feature. This feature automatically saves your work at regular intervals to a temporary location on your computer. If an unexpected crash or closure occurs, you can often recover your document from this location.

To access AutoRecover in Office applications:

- Open the respective Office application.
- Click on "File" and select "Open."
- In the sidebar, you'll see a list of recent documents, including any recovered versions with " (when I closed without saving)" in the title. Click on the document to open it.

It's essential to regularly save your work manually as AutoRecover intervals might not capture every change.

2. Backup Your Office Documents

Creating regular backups of your important Office documents is a proactive approach to data loss prevention. Here are some methods to consider:

- **File Backup**: Use built-in or third-party backup tools to schedule regular backups of your documents. You can set these tools to automatically back up your files to an external drive or cloud storage.

- **Cloud Storage**: Save your Office documents to cloud storage services like OneDrive or Google Drive. These services offer automatic versioning, allowing you to recover previous versions of your documents.

- **Email Backup**: Send important documents to yourself as email attachments. This provides an additional copy of the document in your email account.

3. Data Recovery Software

In cases of accidental deletion or data loss, data recovery software can often retrieve lost Office documents. These applications scan your storage devices for deleted or lost files and attempt to recover them.

Popular data recovery software includes EaseUS Data Recovery Wizard, Recuva, and MiniTool Power Data Recovery. Follow the instructions provided by the chosen software to initiate the recovery process.

4. Preventing Data Loss

Preventing data loss is often more effective than trying to recover lost data. Consider the following practices:

- **Regularly Save Your Work**: Manually save your documents frequently, especially after making significant changes.

- **Use Version Control**: In collaboration scenarios, enable version control features in Office applications. This allows you to track changes and revert to previous versions if needed.

- **Employ Document Protection**: Password-protect sensitive documents to prevent unauthorized access and changes.

- **Automated Backup**: Set up automated backup solutions to ensure your data is regularly backed up to an external location.

- **Train Users**: In business settings, educate employees about data loss prevention strategies and best practices.

By implementing these strategies and combining data recovery tools with proactive prevention measures, you can significantly reduce the impact of data loss incidents. Always remember that prevention is key, but having recovery tools and practices in place provides an additional layer of security for your valuable Office documents.

Chapter 20: The Future of Microsoft Office

In this final chapter, we'll explore the exciting developments and future trends in Microsoft Office. As technology continues to evolve, so does the Office suite. Microsoft is continually working on enhancing Office applications, embracing new technologies, and adapting to changing user needs.

Section 20.1: Emerging Trends in Office Productivity

Office productivity is undergoing a transformation, driven by emerging trends that reshape the way we work, collaborate, and use Office applications. Here are some of the prominent trends shaping the future of Office:

1. Cloud Integration

The cloud is becoming increasingly central to Office productivity. Office 365 and cloud storage services like OneDrive and SharePoint enable seamless collaboration, real-time document editing, and access to your work from anywhere, on any device.

2. AI and Machine Learning

Artificial Intelligence (AI) and Machine Learning (ML) are poised to play a significant role in Office applications. Expect smarter assistance, predictive typing, data analysis automation, and improved document summarization.

3. Enhanced Collaboration

Collaboration tools within Office applications are evolving. Expect more robust real-time co-authoring, better integration with chat and video conferencing, and easier sharing and commenting on documents.

4. Accessibility and Inclusivity

Microsoft is committed to making Office applications more accessible for everyone. Look for improved accessibility features, such as inclusive design, voice commands, and AI-driven assistance for users with disabilities.

5. Hybrid Work Environments

As remote and hybrid work arrangements become commonplace, Office applications will adapt to support flexible workflows. Features like Teams and cloud-based collaboration will continue to facilitate remote teamwork.

6. Security and Privacy

With the increasing importance of data security and privacy, Office will continue to enhance its security features. Expect advanced encryption, data loss prevention, and tools to help organizations meet compliance requirements.

7. Integration with Emerging Technologies

Office applications will integrate with emerging technologies like Augmented Reality (AR) and Virtual Reality (VR). Imagine creating 3D presentations or collaborating in virtual environments.

8. Subscription Model and Frequent Updates

The move towards subscription-based licensing ensures users receive regular updates and new features. Microsoft will continue to deliver fresh capabilities to Office 365 subscribers.

9. Customization and Extensibility

Customization will be key. Users and organizations will be able to tailor Office applications to their specific needs, creating custom add-ins and solutions using tools like Office Add-ins and SharePoint Framework.

10. Data Insights and Visualization
Office applications will provide more robust data analysis and visualization capabilities. Power BI integration and enhanced charting tools will enable us ers to derive insights from data more effectively.

The future of Microsoft Office is promising, with a focus on improving productivity, collaboration, and accessibility. Embracing these emerging trends will empower users to work smarter, adapt to changing work environments, and make the most of Office's evolving capabilities. As technology continues to advance, Microsoft Office will remain a vital tool for individuals and organizations worldwide.

Section 20.2: AI and Machine Learning in Office

Artificial Intelligence (AI) and Machine Learning (ML) have become integral components of Microsoft Office, revolutionizing the way users interact with these applications. These technologies are poised to play an increasingly significant role in enhancing productivity, automating tasks, and providing intelligent assistance across the Office suite.

AI-Driven Assistance

AI-powered features are already improving user experiences in Office applications. For example, in Microsoft Word, AI-driven suggestions for grammar and style help users write more effectively. In Outlook, AI helps prioritize emails and suggests replies, saving time and reducing email overload. These capabilities will only continue to improve as AI algorithms become more sophisticated.

Predictive Typing

One exciting application of AI in Office is predictive typing. As you compose emails or documents, AI can predict what you're likely to write next based on your previous writing patterns. This feature can save time and reduce keystrokes, making your work more efficient.

Data Analysis Automation

In Microsoft Excel, AI is transforming data analysis. Excel's AI features can identify trends, outliers, and anomalies in your data automatically. It can also suggest relevant charts and pivot tables to visualize your data effectively. This empowers users to derive insights from their data more easily, even if they're not data experts.

Document Summarization

AI-powered document summarization is another exciting development. In the future, Office applications may offer the ability to automatically generate concise summaries of lengthy documents. This can be immensely useful for quickly grasping the key points of reports, articles, or research papers.

Natural Language Processing

Natural Language Processing (NLP) is at the core of AI-powered features in Office. It enables applications to understand and respond to natural language input. Imagine conversing with Office applications in plain English, asking questions, and receiving meaningful answers. This is becoming a reality thanks to NLP advancements.

Enhanced Translation

AI-driven translation capabilities are making Office more accessible to users around the world. Real-time translation of documents and conversations in Microsoft Teams breaks down language barriers, facilitating global collaboration.

Future Possibilities

Looking ahead, AI and ML will continue to shape the future of Office. Microsoft is investing heavily in these technologies to provide users with increasingly intelligent and personalized experiences. Whether you're using Word, Excel, PowerPoint, or any other Office application, expect AI to be there, helping you work smarter and more efficiently.

As these AI and ML features evolve, they will become even more integrated into the Office workflow, offering valuable insights, automating repetitive tasks, and assisting with complex projects. Embracing AI and ML in Office will be essential for staying competitive and maximizing productivity in the modern workplace.

Section 20.3: The Evolution of Cloud Computing in Office

Cloud computing has undergone significant evolution within the Microsoft Office ecosystem, transforming the way users create, store, collaborate on, and access documents and data. This section explores the evolution of cloud computing in Office and its profound impact on productivity and collaboration.

Early Cloud Integration

The journey of cloud computing in Office began with the introduction of cloud storage services like Microsoft's OneDrive and SharePoint. These services allowed users to store their documents and data in the cloud, making them accessible from anywhere with an internet connection. This marked a significant shift away from traditional local file storage.

Real-Time Collaboration

One of the most transformative aspects of cloud computing in Office is the ability to collaborate in real time. With cloud-based tools, multiple users can simultaneously work on the same document, spreadsheet, or presentation. This real-time collaboration has revolutionized the way teams collaborate and has become essential in the era of remote work.

Seamless Cross-Platform Access

Cloud computing has enabled seamless access to Office applications and documents across various devices and platforms. Whether you're using a Windows PC, a Mac, a smartphone, or a tablet, you can access your Office files and work on them with ease. This flexibility enhances productivity and empowers users to work from their preferred devices.

Automatic Syncing and Version Control

Cloud-based storage ensures that your documents are automatically synced across all your devices. Changes made on one device are instantly reflected on others. Additionally, version control is simplified, as cloud services maintain a history of document changes, allowing users to revert to previous versions if needed.

Cloud-Powered AI and ML

The cloud also serves as the foundation for AI and ML capabilities in Office applications. These cloud-powered features, such as grammar and style suggestions in Word or intelligent data analysis in Excel, rely on cloud-based AI models that continuously improve and adapt.

Enhanced Security and Compliance

Cloud computing in Office has led to enhanced security and compliance features. Data stored in the cloud is often subject to robust encryption, authentication, and access control measures. This is crucial for safeguarding sensitive information, particularly in industries with stringent compliance requirements.

Evolving Integration

As cloud computing continues to evolve, Office applications are becoming more deeply integrated with cloud services. Features like automatic backup to the cloud, real-time chat and collaboration in Microsoft Teams, and cloud-based add-ins are examples of this integration.

Future of Cloud Computing in Office

The future of Office is intrinsically tied to the cloud. Microsoft's commitment to cloud-first development means that we can expect more innovation and integration with cloud services. This includes improvements in AI and ML capabilities, enhanced security measures, and greater flexibility for users to work from anywhere.

In conclusion, cloud computing has brought about a paradigm shift in the way we use Microsoft Office. It has made collaboration more accessible, improved data accessibility, and enabled powerful AI-driven features. As cloud technology continues to evolve, so will the capabilities of Office applications, ensuring that users can work smarter and more efficiently in an increasingly connected world.

Section 20.4: Office in the World of Virtual and Augmented Reality

Virtual Reality (VR) and Augmented Reality (AR) are rapidly emerging technologies that are poised to have a significant impact on the future of Microsoft Office. This section delves into the potential applications of VR and AR in the Office environment and explores how these technologies are reshaping the way we work and collaborate.

Virtual Reality in Office

VR has the potential to revolutionize the way we conduct meetings and collaborate remotely. Imagine stepping into a virtual meeting room where you and your colleagues, regardless of their physical locations, can interact in a lifelike environment. VR can offer immersive presentations, training sessions, and brainstorming sessions, providing a sense of presence that traditional video conferencing cannot match.

One of the applications gaining traction is the use of VR for data visualization. Users can step into 3D representations of complex data sets, gaining insights that are difficult to grasp from traditional 2D charts and graphs. This can be especially valuable in fields like data analysis and scientific research.

In addition to meetings and data analysis, VR can enhance training and onboarding experiences. New employees can immerse themselves in virtual environments that simulate their workspaces, making the learning process more engaging and effective.

Augmented Reality in Office

Augmented Reality, on the other hand, overlays digital information on the physical world. In the context of Office applications, AR can provide hands-free access to information while working. For example, wearing AR glasses, a technician can receive real-time instructions while repairing a complex piece of equipment, with relevant schematics and data overlaid on their field of view.

AR can also facilitate remote assistance scenarios, where an expert can guide a field worker through a task by annotating their live view with instructions and diagrams. This has applications in industries ranging from manufacturing to healthcare.

Another use case for AR in Office is enhanced productivity. Users can create virtual sticky notes, annotations, or reminders that are location-based. For example, you could leave virtual notes on your desk or mark specific pages in a physical document with digital highlights.

Microsoft's HoloLens and Mixed Reality

Microsoft's HoloLens is a pioneering device that brings mixed reality (a combination of VR and AR) to the workplace. It allows users to interact with holograms in their real-world surroundings. In an Office context, HoloLens can enable engineers to visualize and manipulate 3D models, architects to walkthrough virtual buildings, and educators to create immersive learning experiences.

Microsoft has already introduced applications like Dynamics 365 Remote Assist and Layout, which leverage HoloLens for remote collaboration and design reviews.

The Future Outlook

While VR and AR are still in the early stages of adoption in the Office environment, their potential is vast. As hardware becomes more affordable and accessible, and software applications become increasingly sophisticated, we can expect to see broader integration of these technologies into the everyday workflows of Office users.

In conclusion, VR and AR are opening up new frontiers in how we interact with and utilize Microsoft Office. They have the potential to enhance collaboration, training, data analysis, and productivity in ways that were once the stuff of science fiction. As these technologies mature, they are likely to play a central role in the future of Office applications, shaping the way we work, create, and connect.

Section 20.5: Preparing for Future Office Updates and Changes

In the ever-evolving landscape of technology, staying prepared for future updates and changes to Microsoft Office is crucial for maintaining productivity and ensuring a seamless transition to new features and functionalities. This section explores strategies and best practices for anticipating and adapting to future changes in the Office suite.

Embrace Cloud-Based Services

One of the significant shifts in recent years has been the move towards cloud-based services within Office 365. As Microsoft continues to invest in cloud technologies, it's essential to embrace these services fully. This includes utilizing OneDrive for cloud storage, SharePoint for collaborative workspaces, and Teams for real-time communication and collaboration. Cloud-based services provide flexibility, scalability, and easier access to updates and new features.

Stay Informed

Microsoft regularly releases updates, patches, and new features for Office applications. To stay informed about these changes, consider the following:

1. **Official Microsoft Resources**: Microsoft maintains official websites, blogs, and newsletters dedicated to Office updates. Subscribing to these resources can keep you up to date with the latest news and feature announcements.

2. **User Communities**: Joining Office user communities and forums can provide valuable insights into how others are adapting to updates. It's a platform to ask questions, share experiences, and learn from the community.

3. **Training and Learning Resources**: Microsoft offers various training and learning resources, including online courses and documentation. These resources can help you quickly adapt to new features and changes.

Test Updates in a Controlled Environment

Before rolling out Office updates or changes to your entire organization, it's wise to test them in a controlled environment. Create a testing group within your organization to evaluate how updates may impact your specific workflows and processes. This allows you to identify and mitigate potential issues before a widespread deployment.

Plan for Training and Adoption

New features and changes in Office applications often require some level of training and adaptation. It's essential to plan for user training and adoption strategies to ensure a smooth transition. Consider the following:

1. **Training Programs**: Develop training programs or workshops to introduce users to new features and changes. These programs can be conducted in person or virtually.

2. **User Guides and Documentation**: Create user-friendly guides and documentation that explain how to use new features. Provide easy access to these resources.

3. **User Support**: Offer user support channels where employees can seek assistance or ask questions related to the changes. This can include help desks, chat support, or dedicated support personnel.

Customize Office to Your Needs

Microsoft Office allows for a significant degree of customization. You can tailor the suite to meet your organization's specific needs and preferences. Explore options for customizing the Office ribbon, creating templates, and using macros to automate tasks. Customization can enhance productivity and adapt Office to your unique workflows.

Prepare for Security and Compliance

As Office continues to evolve, so do security threats and compliance requirements. Stay proactive in addressing security concerns by implementing robust security measures, such as multi-factor authentication and data encryption. Ensure that your organization complies with relevant regulations, especially if you handle sensitive data.

Feedback and Collaboration

Microsoft values user feedback and often incorporates user suggestions into updates and changes. Encourage your organization to provide feedback through official channels. Additionally, consider collaborating with Microsoft or third-party developers to build custom solutions that align with your specific needs.

In conclusion, preparing for future Office updates and changes requires a proactive approach. Embrace cloud-based services, stay informed, test updates, plan for training, customize Office, address security and compliance, and actively engage in feedback and collaboration. By following these strategies, you can navigate the evolving Office landscape with confidence and ensure that your organization remains productive and competitive.

www.ingramcontent.com/pod-product-compliance
Lightning Source LLC
Chambersburg PA
CBHW071038290526
45795CB00004B/1215